CW00394375

Romney Marsh

IN OLD PHOTOGRAPHS

Douglas Oiller, coxswain of the Dungeness lifeboat, pictured in 1933. He was coxswain at Dungeness for thirty-one years until his retirement in 1947, and was awarded the RNLI Bronze Medal for his part in the service to the barge *Marie May* on 12 November 1929.

Romney Marsh

IN OLD PHOTOGRAPHS

EDWARD CARPENTER

Alan Sutton Publishing Limited
Phoenix Mill · Far Thrupp · Stroud
Gloucestershire

First Published 1994

British Library Cataloguing in Publication Data.
A catalogue record for this book is available from
the British Library.

ISBN 0-7509-0653-7

Typeset in 9/10 Sabon.
Typesetting and origination by
Alan Sutton Publishing Limited.
Printed in Great Britain by
Ebenezer Baylis, Worcester.

Copyright © Edward Carpenter, 1994

*To Margaret Bird, without whose
friendship, generosity, patience, advice
and hard work this book would not have
been written.*

Contents

The Tower of Lydd Church about 1925. From a distance the dignified 132-foot tower, raised in 1442 by Thomas Stanley at a cost of £280, stands out majestically from the flat fertile acres of the Marsh. The car standing by Goble's Tearooms is probably a De Dion Bouton.

Introduction

Romney Marsh, both gifted and wrested from the sea over a period of more than a thousand years to form Kent's historically labelled 'Sixth Continent' of the world, has a character all its own. This character is derived in part from the fierce independence of the men and women who helped create it. Time, however, does not stand still and recent decades have wrought big changes in the social and economic patterns and landscape of the Marsh. The photographs in this book, all taken between 1860 and 1936, have been chosen to illustrate and commemorate a way of life now lost for ever.

Romney Marsh is the collective name of four distinct marshes: Romney Marsh proper, Walland Marsh, Dengemarsh and, just over the border in Sussex, Guldeford Marsh. The photographs cover an area running from the River Rother in the west to the Grand Redoubt, West Hythe, in the east; and inland bordered by the Royal Military Canal, dug as a defence against a feared Napoleonic invasion. These flat green pastures with their rich alluvial soil have been the envy of graziers the world over, giving their name to a breed of sheep with the longest traceable pedigree in England, the Romney. Today, though, because of the decline in the sheep industry, two-thirds of the Marsh is under the plough, growing bumper crops of cereals, potatoes and oilseed rape.

Many of the photographs are previously unpublished and portray a quieter, more relaxed way of life than now, even though a harder one. It was a time when farming was still labour-intensive; when the small towns and villages were largely self-contained; when each village had its own shops and artisans; when the stores of Lydd and New Romney could provide every want, from a bootlace to a bicycle, or even a tailor-made suit; and when the tradespeople were happy to deliver their goods to the outlying farmsteads and the coastal fishing communities. Men either walked or cycled to work, while the better-off farmers travelled by pony and trap. Horses reigned supreme until the advent of cars and vans and the mechanization of farms; and many Marsh dwellers never ventured over the borders of their 'Continent'.

The establishment of a permanent Army camp at Lydd in 1881 brought not only new job opportunities for the Marshmen but also resulted in the building of a railway line, principally to transport troops to the ranges. There had been an Army presence in the town since 1879, though mainly Territorials in the summer months.

Lydd was also the home of an Advanced Balloon School, of which there were only two in the country, the other being at Larkfield, also in Kent. The Royal Flying Corps had an airfield at the Derings, Lydd and one at Jesson (now St Mary's Bay), referred to as Dymchurch airfield, while along at

Camber a Mr A. Ogilvie built his own private aircraft and flew it on the Camber sands.

The Royal Navy was represented by the Coastguard, stationed at intervals along the coast from the Redoubt at West Hythe as far as the River Rother at Rye Harbour, and it was coastguards who manned the first lifeboat in 1826, at Tower 27 Jesson (St Mary's Bay). Dungeness acquired a lifeboat in 1854 followed by Littlestone in 1871. Until 1906 both boats were crewed by coastguards as well as local fishermen, and both won renown for carrying out daring sea rescues, sometimes at the cost of lifeboatmen's lives. Dungeness still has an offshore boat and Littlestone an inshore one.

To save lives, and property, on land, the Lydd Volunteer Fire Brigade was formed in 1890 to serve the whole of Romney Marsh. Brigades for Dymchurch and Camber came forty-six years later in 1936.

Fishing was always the Marsh's secondary occupation, with the main fishing fleet berthed at Dungeness from where it was operated by the Tart, Oiller, Richardson, Haines and Thomas families, who still fish from there today. To the west there were boats at Rye Harbour; the Southerdens had kettlenets at the Midrips, Jury's Gut; the Tart family lived at and sailed from The Brooks until that area was requisitioned by the Army, when they joined the Freathys at Galloways; and one of the oldest fishing families was that of the Prebbles at Dengemarsh. To the east were a few boats manned by the Sharpes and Barnes at Littlestone, and the Henley and Smith families fishing from Dymchurch.

At this time, too, the natural attraction of beaches and sand, particularly at Dymchurch and Camber, began to breach the insularity of Romney Marsh, attracting growing numbers of road- and rail-borne day-trippers and leading soon to the setting up of holiday camps for visitors from all parts of the country.

Many other changes have taken place since the period of this book's photographs, some for the better and some for the worse. Health, housing, education and transport have improved, but the once vital local trades – blacksmith, wheelwright, carpenter, cobbler – have all but vanished, along with many village shops and some village schools; fishing has declined and small farms have been swallowed up.

Old customs are dying in the face of a faster, noisier and less picturesque world. May the photographs in this book serve as an affectionate reminder of what has been lost.

Edward Carpenter, 1994

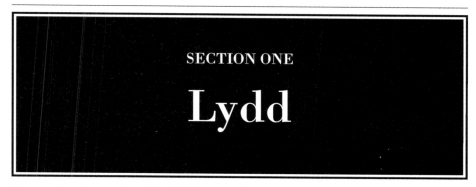

SECTION ONE
Lydd

The ancient borough of Lydd, lying at the southernmost boundary of Romney Marsh, is dominated by the oldest and largest of the Marsh churches, dating back in part to Saxon times and known as the Cathedral of the Marsh. A German bomb in 1940 caused it serious damage, but so well has it been restored by the people of Lydd that no visible scars remain.

The pictures which follow suggest Lydd has suffered little modernization as compared with neighbouring towns and villages. Lydd's main loss has been in prosperity since the period covered by the illustrations. This is largely due to the absence of a permanent Army garrison in the town, or a successor to the Royal Flying Corps of those earlier days, and the closure of the town's brewery, the two cinemas and a number of businesses.

However, Lydd's community spirit – the envy of others – remains, as does its pride in its history, exemplified by an excellent museum housed in the old fire station where it is funded and managed by local enthusiasts.

The Cathedral of the Marsh, *c.* 1920. It is the oldest church on Romney Marsh and has the tallest tower and the longest nave of any parish church in Kent.

A bird's-eye view of Lydd High Street, *c.* 1885. Looking down from Lydd's church tower to the High Street one cannot fail to notice the large new brewery built by Edwin Finn & Sons, where their excellent quality family ales were produced. Along the High Street the pattern of the roofs has not altered to this day, even though considerable changes have taken place to the shop fronts.

The town and camp in 1885. This view of the Army camp and the sea shows the huts of 'Tin Town' (galvanized Army huts) and the permanent buildings of the Lee Metford Camp, beyond which can be seen the white tents of the Summer Camps used by the Territorials. Immediately in the foreground are the crossroads then known as Wheeler's Green, but re-named Coronation Square at the crowning of Edward VII.

From the tower, looking east in 1881. In this view can be seen several thatched roofs which were common at this time. Elm trees abounded, sadly now lost to disease. The Smockmill stands out on the East Rype where the new cemetery is now. One can see that the sails are turning on the mill, which was to be destroyed by fire in 1927. The newly built railway station can just be spotted at the top left of the photograph.

An early photograph of Lydd High Street, c. 1860, showing the rough unmade road and the newly completed brick paths laid after many complaints. They provided a considerable improvement for pedestrians, especially during the winter months. New Hall on the left is seen here as a shop, the owner being one Charles Allen; it is now a house. Next to it is the George Hotel, trying to forget the events of a short time before, when a Revenue Officer was murdered by the local people. Next come the Guild Hall and gaol, busy places in times of smuggling, and even further down on the left of the picture we can see Cobb Hall.

Mr Bartram set this scene for his camera, *c.* 1915. This view features the right-hand side of the High Street on an autumn morning: the coastguard and his children, Mr Blacklocks at his shop doorway, the gentleman with his bicycle and the lady with her daughter and child in a pram pause for the photographer before continuing their shopping. On the left a few men can be seen waiting for the George to open. It will be seen that by this date New Hall had become a residence.

Russell's Bazaar, *c.* 1890. Russell's, drapers and general merchants, 'stock all a person wants', claims their advertisement of the time. In 1893 the end part of the building, with the lantern outside, became a branch of Lloyds Bank. Outside the church wall can be seen the village pump (there was no mains water until 1903) with a boy drawing the water. There are gates to the graveyard because the 'Rypers' (sheep) still roamed the town.

Coming from Skinner Road into Coronation Square in 1912. The most noticeable difference now is the Austin's garage site on the right; a small piece of wall remains the same, but otherwise it has been rebuilt. The fenced-in garden is now the garage forecourt. Across the square are the shops of Mr A. White, grocer, draper and general provision merchant, noted for his quality teas, Pink's Jams and Huntley & Palmers Biscuits. Opposite was Smither's forge and ironmonger's shop.

Coronation Square, c. 1920, with its railed garden housing the First World War gun, presented to Lydd for its war efforts. The globes on the gas lantern are being repaired, and one has a better view of White's shops and the line of buildings leading to the High Street. The square faced a fierce 'Clochemerle' controversy in 1918 when there was a proposal to place a public convenience on the site, but opposition was strong enough for the idea to be abandoned.

The pleasant scene of early Station Road, *c.* 1900. On the right can be seen Porch House, an old building which was demolished after the Second World War to be replaced by a bungalow. The weatherboarded cottage with thatched roof and the house next door were destroyed by a bomb during the same war and now four modern houses occupy these sites. On the left stand Inkerman Villas and some elm trees. Looking further down the road, the buildings have altered very little over the years in this now busy thoroughfare.

Proceeding down Station Road, *c.* 1900, we have in front of us the side road leading to the churchyard, while the main road bears to the right past the thatched Oak Cottage into the High Street. On the immediate left, with their tiled porches, are two cottages on which the fronts have been changed; the second now has a large shop window. The two newly built houses which can be seen had only been completed in 1887. Dolly Bond's shop (now a Chinese take-away) can just be seen with the lantern above the door.

New Street, seen here in 1910, was once the main thoroughfare through the town with some of the oldest buildings still surviving. A beer house of Finn's Brewery, The Rising Sun, is on the corner to the left. The site at the rear of the property had been Thomas Haisell's brewery in 1832. This went through several ownerships, eventually being acquired by Finn's in 1874. The Methodist church, built in 1885, replaced an earlier chapel which stood round the corner in Ness Road. Many of the other buildings in New Street are of great interest and range in date from the fifteenth century.

Queen's Road, c. 1900. The garden shed on the left of the photograph was Lydd's first fish and chip shop, run by a Mrs A. Scholl. The food was cooked in coppers of boiling fat, and the shop was open for business on Wednesday, Friday and Saturday evenings. The cottages on the right, built c. 1860, still exist, and retain their 'front doors' at the back. Goble's bakery is at the crossroads (the house on the left with the porch), with the Salvation Army hut opposite – now, of course, the Hardy Hall. Note the lovely hat worn by the lady with the pram.

East gate to the churchyard, *c.* 1910. Children are shown here posing for Mr Shaw, the military photographer. An older girl is out with her younger sisters, with the baby in a Victorian mail cart. The fancy goods shop later became a butcher's shop run by Mr Cliff Cole. Today the scene has altered because a projecting shop front was built in the 1920s for Harmer's Stores, where in this photograph can be seen a shaped holly tree.

The Guild Hall, Lydd, *c.* 1880. This photograph shows the changes this building has undergone. The three railed and arched doorways once protected an open area beneath the Guild Hall where the market and public meetings took place. In 1883 alterations were made to incorporate the old gaol and the railed-in area, making one large building.

SECTION TWO

New Romney

One of the original five Cinque Ports, providing ships and men to defend the Straits of Dover, New Romney has been left stranded by the sea. Although it has lost its former great importance, it still retains its position as capital of Romney Marsh. Much of historic interest remains – notably the twelfth-century church of St Nicholas, the seventeenth-century Assembly Rooms, the Priory House and the John Southland Almshouses.

Littlestone-on-Sea, linking the town with the coast, was destined in the early twentieth century to become an upmarket holiday area for the well-to-do, with large houses dwarfing the small tarred coastguard dwellings and the lifeboat station, and with even a Grand Hotel. But the grandiose vision of entrepreneur Henry Tubbs foundered on the outbreak of the First World War, resulting in today's rather uneasy mix of ancient and modern, size and style.

The entrance to New Romney from Lydd, *c.* 1915. The Cinque Port Arms, displaying the *News of the World* sign, is on the right and further along come Forge House and the forge. The houses and shops on the opposite side were demolished for road widening in the 1960s.

The Church of St Nicholas, *c.* 1880. This church is dedicated to St Nicholas of Myra, the patron saint of sailors. The building is mainly of the Norman and the fourteenth-century Decorated period of Gothic, with the tower in five stages – the two lower stages are Norman, the others being later. To enter this fine church a flight of steps takes you down below the surrounding ground level. The difference in levels is said to be the result of the great storms of the thirteenth century when masses of mud and shingle were thrown inland.

High Street, New Romney, *c.* 1912. This photograph shows, on the right-hand side, the sign and lantern of the New Inn with Plumtree House next door, then Kimbers' butcher's shop, now Oak Hall Surgery. Over on the left-hand side of the road is Walter House and the large property of The Priory. Across the Ashford Road stands what was Neame's shop, now called Aboyne House.

A posed photograph, *c.* 1919. The attention of the soldiers who have turned to face the camera rather gives the game away. A motorcycle and sidecar stand outside Pump House, which was then a garage. Pump House takes its name from the water pump which stood close to where the motorcycle is shown. The barber's pole of James Edwards is shown on the right, next to the wine shop of Mr Cooper, Joe Ellis's Hardware, Nell Kemp's shop, Pope's Wines, and Dowle the shoemakers.

The Old Forge, *c.* 1900, is the small wooden building under the tree past the houses where, at one period, the blacksmith was William Ashdown. On the left, Sole House, with ornate railings, was the home of Dr R.R. Daglish, JP, who at this time was the deputy mayor of New Romney. Sole House was demolished in the late 1950s for road widening.

Looking towards Dymchurch, *c.* 1900. The girls and the shopkeeper obviously delighted in posing for such postcards. The building on the right with the gas lantern was the old Wesleyan chapel, since demolished to make way for the present Methodist church. This different view of Sole House shows how much it narrowed the road.

A closer look at the Wesleyan chapel, *c*. 1910. John Wesley, the founder of Wesleyan Methodism, is said to have come to this part of Kent, later going on to preach at his last open air meeting at Winchelsea where a tree still stands to commemorate his visit. The New Romney chapel was built in 1836 and pulled down in the 1920s. The chemist's shop of Mr Geering is now Lloyd's chemist, having changed hands several times over the years.

A carefully posed picture, *c*. 1915, outside the Ship Inn, showing two policemen, the landlord's dog being very patient, and a farmer with his trap. On the low building between the Ship and Buckhurst House are posters advertising the latest films which were shown in the Concert Room of the Ship Hotel, the entrance being near the posters. Buckhurst House is a fine timbered Wealden-type house, but was greatly altered in the eighteenth century. Opposite is Ivy House, for many years the home of the local medical officer. Probably the best-known was Dr MacMillan.

North Street, *c.* 1920, showing the garage of the Carey Brothers, with motor vehicles outside. This company specialized in haulage, taxis and coaches and in earlier times horse-drawn omnibuses. On the opposite side of the road is the Baptist chapel, still very much alive in New Romney today. It was here the Band of Hope meetings were held. The pastor divided his duties between New Romney and Lydd.

Fairfield Road, *c.* 1905. This picture was taken outside The Prince of Wales, where the boy running to join his friends missed the desired publicity by not stopping. The lady with the pram is standing by Fairfield where sheepfairs were once held; today it has been built on. The house down the road is Fairfield House, and opposite in the walled garden was the large residence of Mabledon, now lost to a housing estate.

The fine Norman tower of the Church of St Nicholas, portrayed in 1910. The Assembly Rooms, built in the early eighteenth century in a nice red brick had an earlier schoolroom at the near end dated 1676. The Cinema sign in evidence was put out on the nights when the Paine family from Lydd came to New Romney to show the latest films.

A winter scene, 1909. Heavy snow fell at the beginning of April, bringing with it freezing temperatures that froze new-born lambs to the ground, and consequently many lambs and sheep were lost. Looking back, the picturesque scenes are remembered more than the tragedies.

Another snow scene, 1909. Icicles hang from the gutters and everyone is dressed for winter. The frozen village pump to the right of the children was fortunately no longer in general use because mains water had recently arrived. The photograph shows the pavements cleared, but the roads impassable.

Station Road, leading to Littlestone, *c.* 1925. The corner shop of Mr Cornes has been replaced in recent years by a housing complex. Station Road has undergone great changes since this picture was taken, the playing fields of Southland's School on the left now house a large new school, many trees have disappeared and the road has been built up on either side.

The tree-lined Avenue, *c.* 1930. This has now been renamed Station Road, which does not have quite the same ring. Greatstone Golf Club House is shown, but was later destroyed by fire.

The Littlestone end of The Avenue, *c.* 1930. This view illustrates the vision of H.T. Tubbs, who planted trees down the sides of the road which led to what he fondly hoped would be a holiday resort for the wealthy. Very few of these trees now survive, some have been lost through Dutch Elm disease, others through housing development and the necessary driveways. A nostalgic scene, recalled only through the eye of the camera.

Arriving at Littlestone from New Romney, 1925. Mr Tubbs's Grand Hotel, certainly the largest on the Marsh, is shown on the left with the Marine Parade, another of his ventures, on the right.

The Marine Parade, *c*. 1900. The Marine Parade seen in its entirety, with beautiful balconies overlooking the sea so that the wealthy could enjoy in comfort and at leisure the benefits of the bracing air. The general public from New Romney were apt to take the air along the beach on a Sunday evening, and gaze upon a scene of candle-lit dinners and fashionable clothes.

The beach at Littlestone in 1900. It was probably too cold for bathing, judging by the coats and hats being worn and the fact that Mr Polhill's bathing huts are pulled high above the sea. The photograph shows the glass shelter erected by the Corporation, the tall water tower of 1890 (now converted to a dwelling), the lifeboat house and the small tarred coastguard cottages.

Littlestone-on-Sea in 1915. The drinking fountain was installed to commemorate the Diamond Jubilee of Queen Victoria in 1887 and survives today, but there are very few bathing huts in existence, a familiar sight on beaches in Victorian times. They had a door at each end and, once the occupier was attired in the all-concealing swimming costume, the hut was pushed into the sea and the bather slipped into the water unseen.

The old coastguard cottages, Littlestone-on-Sea, in 1910. These were the last of the old single-storeyed coastguard dwellings, although once there were seven similar ones around the Romney Marsh coast. The family of Chief Boatman H. Mauyer sit for the camera. Behind them is Sandcroft, the residence built for Lord Gladstone, recently damaged by fire.

SECTION THREE

Dymchurch

Fact and fiction are the two features of the seaside village of Dymchurch. The fiction is that it once housed Dr Syn, author Russell Thorndike's daring smuggler parson, hero of books and films. The fact is the massive Dymchurch wall which prevents the hungry sea engulfing not only the village but also the low-lying Marsh behind. Even today the old local saying 'God save the Country, long live the King, but watch the wall', is just as relevant.

With The Street that bisects the village now part of the busy A259, the peaceful scenes depicted below are just a memory recorded by the camera. But despite considerable alterations made in 1821, the small Church of St Peter and St Paul retains many of its Norman characteristics; and New Hall, built nearby in about 1580, is still the headquarters of the traditional Lords of the Level and the meeting place of the bailiff and jurats.

Modern Dymchurch's role is that of a popular little holiday resort blessed with safe and extensive sands.

The village of Dymchurch, 1900, in a view taken from the Martello Tower, showing the main street and the Dymchurch windmill in the background. The mill, which was built in 1829, stood in Mill Road and last worked about 1882.

Coming from the sea wall, *c.* 1910, and looking down the street towards New Romney. The road leading back towards the right takes one to Hythe. The fenced-in garden was destined to be redeveloped and later became a garage and cycle shop. On the left is the coastguard station of 1908.

The Street, *c.* 1915. At this time a horse's gait set the maximum speed of the traffic, and compared to the speeds of the present day this must have been very peaceful. The tall building, to which two more were added later, belonged to the Smith family as a general store. The horse in the middle distance is heading for the New Romney road; to the right is Mill Road.

The Arcade and Marine Terrace, c. 1920. From the house called St Joan, Marine Terrace, Russell Thorndike wrote his Dr Syn saga. Now the ground level of the terrace has nearly all been made into shops. An arcade still exists, although the one shown was destroyed by a bomb during the Second World War. On the other side of the road, where one can see a charabanc, was and still is the bus station.

The centre of Dymchurch, c. 1935. The picture shows the central Cycle Stores and Garage of Ernest Wraight, and the Arcade run by Arthur Geering. Both buildings were destroyed by a bomb on 24 August 1940, but both have been rebuilt on similar lines. Opposite is Cooper's Stores and there is a sign for the nearby car park where one could leave one's vehicle all day for sixpence (2½p).

The Bus Station and the Central Restaurant, *c*. 1925. The large dining area of the latter was well able to seat the visitors who came to Dymchurch, attracted by the safe sands. The tall building attached to the restaurant was used as a cinema and was run by the Paine family of Lydd. All of this area suffered severe damage from the bombing on 24 August 1940.

A winter scene in 1909, showing Grove House which stood where Norton's Garage (Checksfields) is today on the A259. Looking across to the sea wall we see the boathouse and the rocket apparatus building belonging to the coastguard.

The Victoria Inn, *c*. 1910, was one of the beer houses belonging to Edwin Finn & Sons of Lydd. It was purchased in 1886 with five bedrooms, two bars, a private sitting room, kitchen and cellar. There was also a stable with a yard open to the street. Mrs C. Swift held the licence to this inn for forty-five years.

A later photograph of the Victoria Inn, *c*. 1930, showing its relative position in Dymchurch. The building had become a great deal smarter, for by this date Dymchurch had established itself as a popular seaside resort. In 1958 the name of the inn was changed back to its original name of 'The Ocean'.

The largest hotel in Dymchurch, *c.* 1910. At this time the Ship Hotel offered many services apart from accommodation: the finest beers, wines and spirits, open and closed carriages for hire, a charabanc service to New Romney and Hythe, a bowling green, quoits and a lawn tennis court. The proprietor was Fred Binskin.

The City of London in the centre of Dymchurch opened on to the street and also on to the sea wall, as this picture of *c.* 1905 shows. It is said that it took its name from a barge wrecked on the Dymchurch wall in the eighteenth century.

The Dymchurch sands, seen here in 1930, have always been very popular and a safe bathing area. Judging here by the coats and hats the weather on this day was not so popular – a typical August Bank Holiday. On the beach by the slipway can be seen Mr Coker's boat which gave pleasure trips to holidaymakers.

Bathing tents, Dymchurch, c. 1920. The young lady in white, stepping out of Mr Coker's bathing tents to walk down the beach on the coconut matting provided, was able to hire the tent, the matting to protect her feet across the beach to the sand, and a bowl of water to wash her feet on return, all for a modest sum.

Sand-castle competition, *c.* 1930. Such competitions were sponsored by Nestlé and chocolate was awarded for the best castle on any particular day. The poles and netting seen running down to low water were part of the kettlenets of the Henley family.

Piper's caravan site, *c.* 1930. This holiday site, updated today, belonged to E.W. Piper & Sons and was extremely popular during this period, especially with visitors from London. Some of the caravans were made locally in Dymchurch by Ray Smith and Reg Wraight. The site is still popular and remains in the possession of the Piper family.

SECTION FOUR

Marsh Villages

Spotlighting the Marsh villages, the camera again records the great changes that have taken place since early this century. In the name of progress many houses, shops and small industries typical of Marsh life have been lost for ever. But, fortunately, the basic character and charm of the villages has survived, with the spires or towers of their historic churches still acting as landmarks.

Camera shots of the picturesque village of Appledore – often described as the 'North Gateway to the Marsh' – have been included because although the village itself lies just over the Marsh limits, its boundaries extend into it. Also included are the East Sussex village of Camber, long famed for its wide, golden sands, and the pleasing little hamlet of East Guldeford.

Brookland Church, *c.* 1915. Brookland was the largest of the Marsh villages, and has its extraordinary bell tower detached from the church. The church itself dates from the thirteenth century and has many interesting features. On the left of the picture is Brookland School, built in 1873 and once the property of the church. It is one of the two remaining village schools open today, the other being at Brenzett.

High Street, Brookland, *c.* 1890. This early photograph of George Santer's Corn and Flour store also shows his shop next door. Mr Santer had traded from these premises since 1858. The large tree in the background covers the roofs of the continuing line of buildings, two shops and one house. Mr Stapley's shop appears to be in the middle of the road, but in reality a small road led off to the right. On the opposite side of the road the building frontages have changed and today only one shop survives, that of S. Coleman & Sons, Butchers. The building with protruding shop windows on the left, which was once a grocer's, is now known as The Laughing Frog.

High Street, Brookland, *c.* 1915. This later photograph shows quite a difference to Mr Santer's store. Verandas have been added with a pulley at the top for hauling the sacks of corn and flour into the store. The shop with glazed tiles which read 'Bread, Flour and Corn', and the door with a wheatsheaf engraved in the glass, are all visible today. Brookland House, shown here with a young girl at the gate, is entirely the same today apart from the addition of a new fence. All the shops have undergone frontal changes and the house at the very end has been demolished.

The Royal Oak at Brookland, *c*. 1920, the largest of the three public houses in the village, was owned at this time by Style & Winch Ltd of Maidstone. The visible changes that the Royal Oak has undergone today are all at ground level; the garages on the right are now a bar entrance, the main entrance is now a window, and a new door to the left is another bar entrance. On the left of the picture can be seen the old slaughter-houses.

The Church of St Mary-in-the-Marsh, in 1902. This is one of the most delightful churches on the Marsh, of Norman origin, but mainly Early English in style. As in the case of many of the Marsh churches St Mary's is built on a man-made mound because of a fear of flooding. Here in this peaceful setting lies the grave of the children's author Edith Nesbit who wrote *The Railway Children*. In the picture men are carrying out work to the spire using ladders.

The Fleur-de-Lis, *c*. 1925. The pub stands on the crossroads at Brenzett – a busy road and a large roundabout today. Apart from the bricking-up of the corner door because of the volume of traffic, the building's exterior remains unchanged today. Behind the pub, where the car can be seen, is Russell House where Ernest Moore had his butcher's shop. Across the road is Forge House; the forge itself was just to the left. Further towards Snargate are the three Hethon cottages.

Brenzett Stores in 1910. At the time of the photograph this store belonged to George Capeling and was a general store for most requirements. He was also agent and seed grower for Hadfield's seeds and fertilizers. The nearest end-of-rank of the lovely old weatherboarded cottages housed the post office. Brushwood faggots were used in the garden and for fire-lighting, especially in old ovens; another important use was in sea defences. Today the stores, incorporating the post office, and the weatherboarded cottages, have all survived.

The Church of St George, Ivychurch, in 1900. Dedicated to the patron saint of England, this is a large church for such a small village and dates back to the fourteenth century. It is out of the ordinary in having three towers, the large one overlooking the village, a small round tower on the north wall and a tower incorporating the porch. The outside structure has altered little through the years although the small conical leaded spire seen here was removed in 1919.

The Bell inn, *c.* 1910. Close to most of the Marsh churches stood the village inn, where the bell ringers repaired after their labours. In Ivychurch this was The Bell which is closer than most. Once more the picture is very much a posed one, the two farm carts side by side, the drayman pausing with the barrel before making the delivery. The small leaded spire on the church tower can be seen clearly.

The small but picturesque village of Newchurch, seen here *c.* 1920, lies in the centre of Romney Marsh and was mentioned in the Domesday Book. Our scene shows the three ingredients which made for a successful community in a small village, the church, the shop and the pub. The church, dedicated to St Peter and St Paul, dates from the beginning of the thirteenth century.

The village of Burmarsh, *c.* 1912. Clustered around the twelfth-century All Saints Church, the village is situated in a peaceful part of the Marsh. Apart from modern buildings to the left, the view has changed surprisingly little, and the aptly named Shepherd and Crook still offers hospitality. The church hall, dedicated on 24 July 1908, is the building on the left. The two yews in the churchyard have grown considerably in the last eighty years.

Camber in 1930. The main attraction of Camber is, of course, that long expanse of golden sands. It was always a popular place even before the motor car, but in the 1930s access became easier. A Mr Croshaw erected chalets and huts in the dunes and hired them to the holidaymakers. These buildings remained until the Second World War.

Lydd Road, Camber, c. 1928. In this scene looking towards Rye, the road on the left leads on to the sands. The cars bringing the holidaymakers are interesting: the one heading the group, on the dunes side, is a Rover 8, behind is an Austin 7, while a slightly older Austin can be seen in front of the house. The saloon driving towards the camera is probably a Citroen B12.

Post Office, Store and Café, Camber, *c.* 1930, now called The Green Owl. The main road is covered by sand blown from the dunes which can be seen in the distance. The long corrugated building is the church, behind which stands the Memorial Hall and the school, both of which have now gone. There is now the Church of St Thomas on the new Lydd Road and another Memorial Hall. The children are educated at Rye these days.

The Royal William Hotel, Camber, *c.* 1925. The hotel was owned by Finn's Brewery of Lydd and was situated near the golf club, with five bedrooms, a flush WC (from well water), four ground-floor rooms and an external lavatory built of matchboard with corrugated iron roof and matchboard-lined. The landlady at this time was Mrs E.F. Bradley. Today it belongs to the Rye Golf Club and is used as quarters for the staff, while the house next door is the home of the professional.

A view of the village of Snargate, *c.* 1912, taken travelling from Brenzett. The church of St Dunstan stands on an artificial mound and dates back to the thirteenth century, its tower being built in two stages at around the same period. Of great interest to visitors is the wall painting in the north aisle, that of a great ship of about the year 1500. The noted author of the Ingoldsby Legends, the Revd R.H. Barham, was curate here in 1817. In front of the church the row of cottages was once the Poor House. The man in the road with the wheelbarrow is heading towards the Red Lion inn and the end house of the two which stood beside the Red Lion can just be seen. These houses were demolished some years ago.

Appledore Church in 1900 – a real picture postcard scene. This is the first view of Appledore as you follow alongside the Military Canal from the Marsh. The ivy was removed from the walls in 1909 when work was carried out on the masonry.

Appledore, *c.* 1905. This view was taken from the fields along the military road from Rye, and it would be very difficult to recreate the same scene today because of the development of houses. Nevertheless, little has altered since the photograph was taken.

Appledore Village, *c.* 1900. The history of this village can be traced back to the early date of AD 892 when it was attacked by the Danes. The church is dedicated to St Peter and St Paul and the base of the tower is reputed to be part of an old fort. In the 1930s The Red Lion Inn, owned by Style & Winch, was pulled down and replaced by the present building. Today, the house to the right has lost its balcony and some of the windows have been altered.

The Coast

The coast of the Romney Marsh starts in the west at the River Rother and continues to the Redoubt at Hythe in the east. Along this stretch of coast there were several small fishing hamlets, such as Galloways and Dengemarsh, each apparently supporting its own pub, a fishing family and a coastguard station, all dominated by the main peninsula of Dungeness. Littlestone has been included with New Romney, while Dymchurch is featured individually as a town in its own right.

There were well-known families at Dungeness – the Tarts, Oillers, Richardsons, Thomases and Haines. They are still there today and many are still fishing. Before the road was built connecting Dungeness and Littlestone there were small tarred cottages, The Ship Inn and The Jolly Fisherman. From 1927, with improved roads, the coast became much more of a development area.

Rye Harbour, *c.* 1906. This is the beginning of the Romney Marsh coastline as we know it, the Camber side of the River Rother. The Rye tram station can be seen in the centre of the picture and the tracks indicate the route towards Camber sands. Sailing boats and trawlers are at anchor in the harbour and on the Rye Harbour side can be seen the trucks on the main railway line, opened in 1858, that ran as far as the village.

The British Sailor inn, at Galloways, about two miles west of Dungeness, is thought to have been a cottage for coastguards stationed here as early as 1832. At the time of the photograph, *c.* 1936, this pub was the home of the Freathy family, local fishermen, and one room was used as the bar. A Sunday meal was also served, with a sweet as well – in 1914 the charge was 4*d.*

Dengemarsh, *c.* 1936. When this picture was taken, Dengemarsh was a small fishing hamlet where the long-established family of Prebbles lived. The three cottages were built on the bank known as Pen Bars and were reached by the causeway that the delivery cart is using. The families were forced to move to Lydd during the Second World War.

The Hope & Anchor inn, at Dengemarsh, c. 1930. It was acquired by Finn's Lydd Brewery in 1879 but was probably an inn long before that. It was a timber-built bungalow of four bedrooms, sitting room and the large living room which was used by the public, with a serving bar. It was fully licensed, and the licensee in 1921 was Mr R. Freathy.

Dungeness in 1932, looking towards the north. The little cottage, Spion Kop, with the cart track at the rear, was the home of Jerry Bates. There were no roads in Dungeness at this period and today the cottages are even further from the receding sea.

The scattered cottages of Dungeness, *c.* 1920. This shows the tracks across the beach from one cottage to another, and to the lighthouse, passing the low light and foghorn seen at top left. The first cottage belonged at this time to Twosign Richardson and was called The Cabin, with the goat and chicken houses to the left. The next house, Southview, was the home of Tom Richard Tart, father of the present T.R. Tart, known as Ben, the well-known ex-coxswain of the Dungeness lifeboat.

Setting up home, *c.* 1920. Many people bought disused railway carriages after the First World War and established them at Dungeness as holiday cabins. These were brought down by train, and with the help of rollers and plenty of brawn, were put in place. A ground rent was paid to the Southern Railway.

The cabins, *c.* 1930, in the shadow of the 1904 lighthouse. It is hard to recognize some of the cabins today, as extensions have been added through the years.

The Dungeness cart, *c.* 1936. Because of the lack of roads at Dungeness which only had beach tracks, a special cart with wide wheels was designed very many years ago. The photograph shows Charles Mannering making a delivery to The Britannia inn at Dungeness. Albert (Joss) Jones is the man on the cart. At the time this picture was taken there were two such carts in use, one of which survives and is now on show in the Lydd Museum.

The Pilot inn, *c*. 1910. This is a rear view of the original Pilot inn at Dungeness. It stood on the left side of the road as one enters the Dungeness Estate. This was a fully licensed inn of timber construction with three sitting rooms, four bedrooms and a cellar, and was run by the Tart family for very many years. In 1957 a new Pilot was built on the main coast road.

The opening of the coast road in 1935. This road runs between Dungeness and Littlestone and was opened by the Mayors of New Romney and Lydd, Major M. Teichman-Derville and Mr G.T. Paine. Prior to this only a rough track existed here.

The Parade, Greatstone, seen here in 1935 with its new concrete road, soon attracted the developers. One, Mr C.E. Andrews, proposed the Greatstone Dunes estate with plots selling at £50. Some of his ideas came into being, but fortunately others did not.

Greatstone in 1936. With better roads and the motor car, the sand dunes and beach at Greatstone soon became a popular holiday area with a holiday camp, shops and holiday bungalows being built.

The Ship inn, Lade, c. 1920. This was another beer house belonging to Finn & Sons of Lydd, a single-storey timber building with three bedrooms, a sitting room, a large room for the public, a beer cellar and an outside wooden closet. In 1920 Mr Oiller had been the tenant for forty years. The present Ship inn was built in 1935 beside the old Ship which was demolished.

Greatstone c. 1925, before the developers were let loose on the place. The Jolly Fisherman was built on the corner shown in the picture, and now the whole place has been redeveloped into what is almost a self-contained village.

Mrs Annie Oiller in 1920. Because of the remoteness of Dungeness at that time, and the lack of a good road, several of the inhabitants took to keeping goats for the milk, and occasionally for meat. A small enclosure close to the cottage was made from driftwood, purely for use at milking time, otherwise the animals roamed the beach, browsing on what meagre herbage they could find. In 1935 a few complaints were made because of the number (about eighty), the damage they were causing to the inhabitants' small gardens, and such things as eating washing on the line and boots left out to dry. Dungeness soon acquired the nickname of 'Nanny Goat Island'.

Mrs Nell Prebble in 1936, milking her goat named Sandy McNab, at Dengemarsh. A handmade yoke was made for use at milking time otherwise, as at Dungeness, these goats roamed the beach area, returning home for milking. Sadly, Sandy McNab was blown up by a mine on 19 October 1941.

Valentine Time? Coxswain Doug Oiller of Ocean View, Dungeness, presents his wife Ellen with a spring flower grown in his little garden, c. 1925. A small box garden was made of driftwood, and filled with earth collected from the nearby ballast workings. The area is now known as the Long Pits.

SECTION SIX

Agriculture

Ever since Romney Marsh was first inned (reclaimed from the sea) the wide, level spread of its rich alluvial soil has governed the daily lives of the Marshmen. It was these open, windswept acres that gave birth to that hardy breed of sheep known throughout the farming world as the Romney, prized both for meat and wool.

In fact in 1572 Lydd established its own town flock of 392 ewes which grazed on the Rypes – land granted to the people of Lydd by the then Archbishop of Canterbury in AD 904 – under the watchful eye of the official Town Looker. Shepherds on Romney Marsh are commonly known as 'lookers', although the original looker who tended the sheep for more than one farmer is now a dying breed.

The sheep, too, no longer reign supreme. With the advent of the Second World War much of the immaculate pasture came under the plough, for crops of wheat, potatoes and, more recently, oilseed rape. Larger, mechanized, farms have meant fewer jobs on the land. The old farming photographs that follow portray a harder, more labour-intensive regime which has vanished in just a few score years.

Mopper Apps in 1909, posing with his dog, crook and Romney Marsh sheep. He was a well-known looker and shearer, coming from an old Marsh family. This scene epitomizes the flat green acres so common to Romney Marsh.

The Gillett shearing gang in 1905, at Tourney Hall, Lydd, working for Charles Bass whose son Ray, on horseback, looks on. Mr Gillett is on the far right, the next young shearer is his son Bill while the man kneeling is Mr Batchelor. They are using hand shears, with another man winding the wool and the young lad marking the shorn sheep with the letter 'B' for Bass.

Jack Haisell pictured here in 1912, shearing at Westbroke, Lydd for Arthur Finn, using a hand-turned Stuart No. 6 Shearing Machine. It was a difficult machine to turn, and the chap turning most likely worked harder than the actual shearer. Jack is shearing the old Marsh way, left to right, or round and round as it was called.

The Stuart 'Little Wonder', c. 1915. This was a two-man shearing machine, with a petrol engine which turned a belt connected to the solid shaft to turn the shearing heads. A water-cooling tank was in the centre and the exhaust pipe was attached to the left-hand upright, consequently the shearer on the left had to put up with the exhaust fumes and shear at the same time. In 1915 the cost of a 'Little Wonder' complete was £35 and it could run all day on a gallon of petrol. All the men are wearing the traditional shearing jumpers.

A shearing family in 1912. Mopper Apps with his wife and son, shearing for the Finn-Kelcey family somewhere on Romney Marsh. Mopper was a familiar figure, with his petrol-driven shearing machine mounted on his cart. Mrs Apps wound the fleeces as the sheep were shorn. The young lad, possibly the farmer's son, poses showing the sheep mark of the farmer; the sailcloth protects them from the wind, and Mrs Apps's bonnet gives her protection from the sun.

A shearing gang at Brockman Farm, East Guldeford, c. 1910, using a Wolseley petrol engine driving a 110-volt electric generator. Six shearing machines were run off this, and it was on trial with Mr B. Hobbs the farmer direct from Wolseley so that his lookers could experiment. It was judged too heavy and cumbersome, as two horses were needed to pull it. The shearer holding the machine is Fred Poole Snr.

It's not as painful as it looks, 1936. Demonstrating how the tails of lambs were cut or docked before the invention of the little red rubber rings. The docking iron would be placed in a bucket of hot coals until it was black hot, then pressed on to the tail until it burned through. It apparently had no serious effect on the lamb, but fortunately this method is now a thing of the past.

Romney Sheep Fair, *c.* 1895. This fair was held annually on 21 August at Fairfield, New Romney. As well as sheep, cattle and horses were sold on this day. The scene captures Mr Adolphus of Reeve & Finn, auctioneers of Lydd, about to accept the final bid. His clerk, seated behind him with a stovepipe hat, confirms the buyer. The owner of the sheep stands in the ring with his looker who probably many hours earlier was driving the sheep to the fair from a good distance away.

A sale of sheep, autumn 1914, on a Marsh farm, conducted by Mr W.B. Hobbs, auctioneer of Ashford, who is taking bids for a Romney ram. His rostrum enables him to see the bidders clearly, and the stick is used to bang the top to seal the final bid. His clerk is seated behind him, but I am not certain what was the role of the gentleman in the long coat and leather gaiters sitting on a padded chair.

Jack Pierce of Brooklands, with his dog Meg, *c.* 1936. Of all the lookers on Romney Marsh he was perhaps the best known. In the annual shearing competitions, he many times won the Derville Cup which was awarded annually for the best shearer. Contestants came from far and wide to enter these competitions. His trained sheep dogs were much in demand. Jack Pierce worked for the Merrick family for over fifty years. Sheep played an important role in the economy of the farm, but methods of doing things have changed considerably this century – hand shears to electric ones, lambing against the elements to intensive lambing units, from Cuffs powders and oils to the modern drugs and sprays, and, of course, no road droving, now large sheep transporters are used. There is no longer the need to sleep in the lookers' huts, the use of the motor car has solved that problem and distance is now no object. The camaraderie that existed between the lookers has diminished through the passing of time, for in those days a looker would work for the same family for very many years and would know his opposite number on a neighbouring farm, so could call for help if necessary.

George Noakes, pictured here in about 1925, was born at Scotney Farm, Lydd, the son of a looker and one of five boys who all became well-known lookers. George became a probationer under his father on the farm of Arthur Finn, that well-known judge of sheep and breeder of Romneys. He then became the looker and after twelve years he moved to Brodnyx Farm, St Mary-in-the-Marsh, where he worked for farmer George Palmer until retirement, serving him for forty-seven years. He is seen here shearing at Brodnyx.

Bill Sims was born at Brookland, the son of Samuel Sims 'Looker and Lamber', and helped his father as soon as he could walk. On leaving school he worked for Frank Finn at St Mary-in-the-Marsh, then began a long career with the Blacklocks family of Lydd, starting at Jaques Court in 1926 and staying there as a looker and stockman for fifty-two years. This photograph shows him in about 1920.

George Elvy began his long career helping his looker father as soon as he was old enough. When he was eighteen he became looker for Harold Body at Snargate. His next position was with the Paine family of Lydd, working for twenty-four years for Claude H. Paine and twenty years for Gordon T. Paine. George has now retired and is in his late seventies but still helps a farmer friend with his sheep, passing on his knowledge and experience to a new generation of lookers. He says that to be a looker you should be born and bred into it, and most of the Marsh lookers fall into this category.

A looker's hut in 1935, or to give it the proper name, a 'Sheep House'. There are only about a dozen huts still surviving here on the Marsh. Three are in reasonable condition, the one in the photograph is at Cutter's bridge, and recently has been restored by John Paine. A few years ago a small group of people led by farmer Denis Cole of St Mary-in-the-Marsh rescued a typical design of hut from Newlands Farm at Midley, near Lydd. It has now been rebuilt on his farm by his son John to the exact design, and using all the existing original material. The work and setting are so authentic that it is difficult to believe that it is not one of the original huts.

Tilling the land at Hope Farm, Snargate, with the old wooden Kent Turnwrest plough, c. 1915. The design remained almost unchanged for six hundred years. Following the plough is Fred Bates, then the farmer at Hope Farm.

Planting the seed in 1912. This seed drilling team at Scotney, Lydd, posed for Frank Mittell, a local photographer. The two horses on the right are pulling harrows to break the clods of earth to form the seedbed; the next pair are pulling the seed drill, and the grey has another harrow for covering the seed.

Autumn cultivating at Snargate, c. 1915, using a Bean Brake or Horse Harrow. This was a wooden frame of tines with two adjustable depth-wheels to ensure you were not going too deep. The two fine workhorses responded to every movement by the ploughman and are typical of those used in agriculture at that time, far removed from the large Shire horses seen today at agricultural shows.

A Fowler steam ploughing engine pictured in 1917. This one belonged to John and Edwin Homewood, brothers, of Wills Farm, Newchurch, both of whom were farmers and agricultural contractors. It would be working with a second engine because two were required for steam ploughing, pulling the plough on cables from one side of the field to the other. The engine shown here was sold for scrap in 1950.

An early tractor, *c.* 1912. Made by Saunderson of Bedford, this 30 hp Universal Tractor had a water-cooled petrol/paraffin engine. The name can just be made out on the cooling tank at the rear. The tractor is ploughing with a two-furrow balance plough, probably a converted horse plough, steered by 'Whiskers' Burt who worked for Charles Bass of Tourney Hall, Lydd.

This is Miss Mary Bates photographed in 1925, having her own picture taken for a change. She was a well-known photographer and some of her work appears in this book; many of her postcards are in great demand by collectors today. Mary Bates was an active worker on the farm, taking many parts, including gathering the hay as seen here.

Another load of hay, off to be stacked at Hope Farm, Snargate, in 1925, with visitors taking a ride on the load and having their photograph taken to reminisce on later. Mary Bates is at the rear of the load.

Delivering the trusses of hay, *c*. 1910, on a Marsh road. The load is most likely bound for the railway station as hay was in great demand in the towns for horse fodder, and the Army required an enormous amount for their horses. The trusses would have been cut from the stack with the hay knife, weighed to a half-hundredweight, and tied. The man with the lead horse could be the farmer or his son, dressed in collar and tie to distinguish him at the destination from his worker with the rear horse.

Helping with the harvest, *c*. 1916, are six soldiers from the Royal Siege Artillery based at Lydd Camp, with Fred Bates in the peak cap at his farm at Snargate, photographed by Mary Bates. During the First World War, because most young men were away at the front, or at least serving in the forces, the government allowed soldiers to volunteer to have leave to help with the harvest. Many local farmers were only too pleased to employ them, as many were men of the soil.

A delightful rural scene in 1920 of a milkmaid milking the home cow in the corner of the farm. It is, of course, a posed picture and was taken by Mary Bates of Snargate. Fanny King, also of Snargate, is thought to be the girl. The home cow supplied milk for the family and, in the lambing season, for feeding the sock lambs.

Lunchtime, 1925. This idyllic scene of 'Whiskers' Burt having his lunch break with his ploughing horses is at Pegwell, near Lydd, the horses obviously also enjoying their nosebags. The sacking jackets draped on their backs suggest a cold morning in the early spring. Whiskers looks more at ease with horses than with tractors.

SECTION SEVEN

Fishing

The sea has played an important part in the history of Romney Marsh – as an intruder to be repelled, as a defence barrier against foreign foes, and as a supplier of food. The trawlers from Rye Harbour and the boats from the beach at Dungeness still strive to wrest a living from the sea, but with different methods and the most modern equipment. The industry as shown in the pictures below was primarily centred on driftnetting; hardly any trawling took place. Mackerel were a principal catch, with the main season from May to July, followed by autumn mackerelling in September. At the end of October inshore herring fishing began and continued until late November, when the spratting season started.

Many of the boats were built locally, especially by Phillips of Rye, while practically all the nets came from Bridport in Dorset where they were made to specification.

Sailing up the River Rother in 1915, to enter Rye Harbour, is the fishing smack *Bessie*, RX11. These boats were considerably larger than those sailing from the beach.

The Tart family pictured in 1935. The original home of the Tarts was at The Brooks, but this was requisitioned by the Army for use as ranges in 1865. This caused the family to move their entire belongings, including the house, by horse and cart to Lydd, and then they fished from Galloways. In the boat from left to right are Doug Oiller, Dick Tart and Frank Tart.

The Freathy brothers also fished from Galloways, the family home until they were moved out by the Army during the Second World War, but they continued to fish from Galloways. Here Frank (left) and Ken Freathy bring their boat ashore after a day's fishing.

Dengemarsh, *c*. 1935. From the left Steve Prebble, Tom Prebble and Leggo (Fred) Freathy wait for the right conditions before launching. The boat, built at Rye in 1908, stands on the skids (greased boards) which were used to help winch boats above the high tide line after fishing.

A small group of fishing boats at Littlestone in 1920. The families of Barnes, Polhill and Sharp had their boats and huts here, and also helped the coastguards to man the Littlestone lifeboat. Charles Sharp, fisherman, was the last coxswain before the station closed in 1928.

Jesson beach in 1910. This is an early picture, before the construction of the sea wall, of what is now known as St Mary's Bay. The groynes and the faggot wall were at that time the only sea defences. The fishing boats belonged to the Henley family of Dymchurch, and in the distance can be seen the Littlestone water tower.

Seine-net fishing, c. 1935, from the beach at Dungeness. This method would be used during the summer months when a watch would be kept for a shoal of mackerel. Once this was spotted a boat put out from the beach, feeding a net out and circling the shoal before returning to the beach. The fishermen would gradually pull the net ashore, hopefully full of mackerel.

Kettlenet Fishing

Kettlenetting, a method of fishing for which the sandy bays on either side of Dungeness Point were ideal, has now ceased. The stands, as they were known, were worked by local families: the Southerdens, Tarts, Gilletts, Blacklocks, Smithers and Paines, while Dymchurch had the Henleys, Smiths and another family of Paines. The heyday of this enterprise was the 1890s through to the 1930s, though the Gilletts continued operating until 1953. Mackerel were the principal target, but a variety of fish were caught, with a season lasting from April to December.

As shown in the pictures, nets were erected on poles rammed into the sand at low tide; first a straight row called the range net, running seawards from the highwater line, then a circle at the end, called the bythe. When the tide rose, covering the netting, passing shoals of fish encountered the range net and instinctively turned out into deeper water, only to be trapped in the bythe. When the tide receded the fish were collected, and if the catch was a good one a basket was hoisted on a pole to alert the members of the family that more carts would be needed.

Why kettlenet? Because as the water dropped the panicking fish in the bythe looked like a kettle on the boil. And from this there derives the saying 'A pretty kettle of fish'.

Teddy Tart puts the net on to the poles at The Brooks, Lydd, *c.* 1915.

The tide has receded and the Southerden family prepare to enter the bythe with the horse and cart at Jury's Gap near Camber in 1912, hoping for a good catch. In the cart would be a draw net and two or more skim nets.

Gathering the harvest of mackerel in 1912, using a small draw net. This was used to split the shoal into smaller and more manageable parts. Two men would draw the net behind the cart, so trapping a number of fish, and then use the skim net to shovel the catch into the cart. Skim nets were rather like large snow-shoes.

A good haul, *c.* 1912, as the Gillet family unload their catch at Dengemarsh. The full cart was emptied above the tide line, to return for more if necessary. Should the catch be too big, the kettlenet would be lifted and the catch released.

In the fish yard at Lydd, *c.* 1915. Once the catch was back at the fish yard, in this case at Lydd, the locals would wash, sort and pack the fish into boxes. The small fish would be sold locally and some herrings would be kept for smoking in the 'Hang' as bloaters or kippers. The mackerel would be put on the train, bound for Billingsgate fishmarket, where the fish salesman would try to get the best price.

The Gillet family in 1912 pose for a photograph before the tide recedes and the work begins. Most of these photographs were taken by Mr Shaw, a local and military photographer, of whom very few pictures exist because he was always behind the camera. Shaw photographs have become highly collectable, and the man himself a somewhat cultish figure so this is an exceptional picture. From left to right seated, Mrs Shaw, Elsie Gillett, Anne Gillett, Mildred Gillett and Mr Shaw standing with his daughter.

A large catch, c. 1920. Sam Southerden and a holiday visitor with a Thresher shark which had been caught in the kettlenets at Jury's Cap. This was not unusual as several large fish are known to have been caught from time to time. On one occasion the horse pulling the cart was bitten on the leg by a similar fish. Fortunately the horse was not badly hurt.

Road and Rail

The coming of the railway to Romney Marsh opened up its horizons as never before. Marshmen had not been great land travellers, and even as late as the mid-twenties the horse was still the principal power for transport for both passengers and goods. Horse-drawn omnibuses ran to the market towns from Lydd and New Romney, and the hotels and livery stables provided horses, wagonettes and dog-carts. Allen's station bus, which plied between Lydd station and the Army camp, is now housed in Lydd Museum.

In 1881 Lydd Railway Company opened a branch line from Ashford to Lydd which within four years was extended to New Romney. A line was also laid to Lydd camp for exclusive use by the Army.

Allen's horse bus in 1911, at Lydd Camp ready to take officers to Lydd railway station.

George Allen's two-horse wagonette in 1908, outside the George Hotel at Lydd, brings the Commissioner of the Levels to the annual meeting. The task of these Commissioners, whose appointment goes back a long way in history, was to safeguard the Marsh families from inundation by the sea. They were responsible for keeping the sea walls in good repair, the waterways free in the sewers (main dykes) and the 'diks' (the small dykes), and collecting the taxes imposed. They would hear a report from the foremen of the various working gangs as to what progress had been made through the year.

Edwin Finn's carriage pictured in 1908. This is a closer look at Edwin Finn's carriage on the same day as the photograph above, and the coachman is Bill Price, Snr. Arthur Finn's carriage is behind with his coachman Mr Day, equally well turned out, and behind them the town bus of George Allen with its passengers, the driver being Justin Smith.

Edwin Finn's brewery dray, *c.* 1912, is shown making a delivery of Finn's Fine Ales to The Duke's Head, Hamstreet, owned by Finns since 1890. The landlord at this time was Clarke Longhurst; the drayman is Mr Caspall of Lydd.

Lydd Goal Running Team, *c.* 1915, is seen leaving Coronation Square for a run at Ivychurch, their banner displayed all the way. The match against Ivychurch would be friendly compared to some teams they played. The wagonette belonged to George Allen.

Engine trouble. This Robey Engine made in 1818 for Godden & Sampson of Lydd, belonged to William Blacklocks of Sycamore House, Lydd. It was sold to W. Blacklocks in 1881 and when returning from New Romney the road, such as it was, gave way at Running Waters and the engine slipped into the dyke. It was recovered with great difficulty. The driver, John Apps, is seen beside the engine in this photograph of 1881.

After a day's threshing in 1895, this 12-ton barrel engine belonging to W. & E. Earl has stopped at Turngates, St Mary-in-the-Marsh, to take on water. The driver is A. Earl, steersman J. Harris Jnr, the man with the oil can J. Harris Snr, Flagman Ned Marshall and the man holding the hose is Tom Marshall, son of Ned.

Smith's Garage, New Romney, *c.* 1920. This card was used by the garage to remind customers or chauffeurs that their cars were due for servicing. The tall open-drive landaulet with the sloping 'coalscuttle' bonnet is a Charron, built about 1907; next is a Vauxhall; LC860 may well be a steam car; then comes a Napier, its neighbour a Mercedes and next a Daimler. The fashion for ladies to wear large hats and men top hats explains why car bodies were so tall.

The garage at St Mary's Bay, *c.* 1925, served Red Line petrol. The white shed displays a gargoyle Mobil oil advertisement on the wall, also cabinets dispensing Texaco and Castrol oils and a Shell petrol pump. The car is a Triumph Super Seven.

This excursion from the Ship Hotel, New Romney in 1920 was possibly a darts club outing. The charabanc in the picture was made by Thornycroft. See how everyone is dressed warmly, all are wearing hats, and there is a hood in case of wet weather. The twin-cylinder motorcycle combination (make uncertain) appears to be part of the outing.

A similar outing from the Royal Mail, Lydd, *c.* 1925, this time in a Daimler solid-tyre open sight-seeing bus. Here it seems to be a men-only outing, and notably there is a member of the Royal Tank Corps in uniform, the Corps being garrisoned in Lydd from 1923 to 1938. The Royal Mail was owned by George Beer & Rigdens of Maidstone, the only pub in Lydd which was not owned by Finns.

Before the roads were tarmacked the potholes in some places were filled with rock chalk, which was not really ideal because it was dusty in summer and the chalk stuck to tyres when wet. This picture, taken in 1920, is obviously posed; the barrows are over-filled so the rocks can be seen, and the men are all looking towards the camera. These men were employed during the winter months when farm work was slack.

The building of better roads was the responsibility of Kent County Council. The road gang laying a new road would follow the roller to sweep any loose grit to one side. Waiting patiently with his horse in 1925 is the carrier C.D. Smith of Brenzett; the front man with the broom is Fred Smith of Old Romney.

In trouble, *c*. 1925. A Super Sentinal steam wagon belonging to the Wingham Engineering Company, and on hire to George Beer & Rigden of Faversham, comes to grief at the Kent Ditch Corner. It was eventually pulled out, unloaded, and taken to Canterbury.

This lorry has fallen victim to the winding, narrow Marsh roads, nearly always running parallel with a dyke. One can look now on this incident of 1925 with a smile as the name on the tailboard was T. DIVER.

One of Carey's Coaches with its driver Mr Fagg. Charles and Frank Carey started a coach service from Littlestone to Folkestone in the 1930s, at first with horse-drawn vehicles. Sadly, in 1952 East Kent took over the service.

The Rye/Camber tram pictured in 1931, showing the petrol locomotive at the Camber Sands station. The tramway ran from Rye, via Golf Links station to Camber Sands.

In this picture, Southern Railway steam locomotive No. 162 is about to depart Dungeness for Lydd in 1929. The line to Dungeness from Lydd was opened on 7 December 1881 for goods only, being upgraded on 1 April 1883 for passengers. In the background the small dwellings are the Trinity House cottages at the foot of the lighthouse.

A view of Lydd station, c. 1915, showing the main line to Ashford, the goods shunting yard, and the line going to Lydd camp, on the left of the picture behind the goods truck. In the top left can be seen The Railway Hotel (now The Bridge Hotel), and left of that is the old police station.

The railway sidings at Lydd Camp, *c.* 1912. This photograph shows the locomotive *Nicholson* arriving from Lydd, while the church can be seen in the background. The line continued beyond the camp in a circular loop as far as The Brooks. It was used extensively by the Garrison Artillery and later by the Royal Tank Corps, and was finally closed in 1927.

The engine *Trafford* at Lydd camp, *c.* 1916, with army crews. The *Trafford* came to Lydd from Manchester and had been built in 1887. There were six locomotives stabled at Lydd, *Nicholson*, *Napier*, *Betty*, *Trafford* and two unnamed. These locos pulled gun trucks, goods and tank trucks as well as two passenger carriages.

The 'smallest public railway' was the claim to fame made by the small railway started in 1925 by Captain J.E.P. Howey, with 15-inch gauge line running from Hythe to Dungeness. It is now the main single holiday attraction on the Marsh and used by many thousands of visitors every year, as well as being in regular service for pupils at Southland's School. The train is seen here entering Dymchurch station.

All aboard for Dungeness, 1927. The train is seen waiting in Dymchurch station, with the booking office on the left. The guard is looking to see that the photographer has got his picture before giving the signal to move.

The Railway Hotel, Lydd, pictured in 1910, was just outside Lydd Town station. The land was leased from the Council and the plans promptly approved so that completion occurred only a year after the railway opened. There were three Railway Hotels in all, at Lydd, Appledore and New Romney. Appledore is the only one retaining its original name – and, indeed, the only one still served by 'real' trains.

A railwayman's trolley, 1912, being used to convey a clergyman to Dungeness to take a service at the old school. To propel the trolley one pushed the centre bar backwards and forwards. Two of the ladies are Edith Bayley and Fanny Bayley, while Gus Bayley sits next to the clergyman.

Lydd Cycle Club have their photograph taken before setting off to Hastings for the day, *c.* 1912. This was no mean feat in those days of solid tyres, fixed wheels, and only the front brake, with roads of nothing like today's standard, although there was nowhere near as much traffic.

Miss Frieda Hobbs, *c.* 1908, in her early years. Miss Hobbs became a well-known and much respected person in New Romney who sadly died in 1993. Some of her collection of photographs grace this book. Her pram, called a Mailcart, a dual-purpose pram, was advertised as suitable for both baby and child and had probably been made by F.W. Oakes of Kidderminster.

SECTION TEN
Windmills

Historians tell us that during the years of the violent storms which changed the shape of Romney Marsh and buried the towns of Old Winchelsea and Broomhill beneath the sea, more than three hundred windmills were lost. Whether they were drainage mills or used to grind corn is not known for certain. What is known is that within living recollection six corn mills existed – three smock, two post and one tower mill, the base of the last being the only reminder now, apart from old photographs and long memories.

Newchurch tower mill is said to have been built by the Revd Nares in 1810, the only tower mill on the Marsh, seen here in c. 1900. The bricks used were from the old rectory when it was demolished. Mr G. Prebble worked this mill from 1893 to 1901. Flour ceased to be produced after 1890, and the mill was then used for grinding farmers' corn. The base of this mill can be seen today.

Lydd post mill, seen here in c. 1890, was one of the finest examples of its type. It was built on the West Rype in 1769, and the Mill Cottage still survives today in Tournay Road, close to the Army camp. As was the fate of many windmills, it mysteriously caught fire and was destroyed in the early hours of 26 February 1900, being virtually burnt out before the alarm was given. At that time it was owned by Thomas Goble.

Lydd smock mill stood in Mill Road near to what is now the new cemetery, and had been completed in 1805 for John Longley. It had various owners through its long history, including the Finn family who owned it for several years. It was sold to Thomas Goble in 1866, and he left it to his son Joseph. In 1922 a 15 hp engine was installed to turn the stones, but times were changing and windmills were becoming uneconomical, and so it fell into decay.

Lydd smock mill on fire in 1927. The fire started while the engine, which had been fitted in 1922, was being dismantled, and despite gallant efforts by the Lydd Volunteer Fire Brigade the mill was completely destroyed. At the time it was still owned by Joseph Goble.

New Romney smock mill, seen here *c*. 1910, stood just out of New Romney on the Dymchurch Road, where the Southlands tennis courts are now. It is believed to have been built around 1769, and Robert Spencer was miller in 1858, while James Stonham worked it from 1878 to 1902. It was then bought by Harold Body who rented it to a Mr Carey. The mill was pulled down in 1920 by Trib Boulden who worked for Harold Body.

Brenzett post mill, pictured in 1905, stood just outside the village on the left-hand side on the road to Snargate. The photograph shows a pleasant rural scene with the little cottage, the miller's three daughters, and the chickens at free range as was the custom, feeding on any corn fallen from the customers' carts. This mill, built in 1776, replaced an even earlier one.

The dismantling of Brenzett mill which occurred because of the escalating cost of repairs and the decline in trade. It was still grinding a small amount for animal feed up to 1924. This picture, taken on 5 February 1925, shows the dismantling gang at work.

Village Shops

At the turn of the century the main village shop was the traditional type selling a little of everything, doubling as the post office, and in one case even repairing bicycles. The family butcher slaughtered animals on his own premises, was well known for his pork sausages and sold pure home-made lard, in bladders or by the pound. A dispensing chemist acted also as a dentist and photographer.

In the small towns grocers became 'Provision Merchants', selling anything from pickles to petrol, squeezing out the smaller traders as do the supermarkets today. Nevertheless, there were still ironmongers, bakers, shoemakers, saddlers, drapers – all important to village viability. Everything bought could be delivered, either by boy on trade bike, or by cart in the near vicinity, or by horse and cart when 'out the grounds' (in the outlying district).

But the shop, above all, was the centre of village life, a place where women (and men) could exchange gossip, learn of births and deaths, discover who was sick and who needed help – a place to put the world to rights.

Lydd post office, seen here in 1905, was owned by Mrs Agnes Butler the postmistress, whose shop was also newsagent, printer and bookbinder, and who produced postcard views of Lydd and New Romney, some of which feature in this book. The gates to the churchyard were to keep out the sheep which roamed the town.

Smithers Ironmongers at 10 Cannon Street, Lydd, facing into Coronation Square. In 1898 the shop was owned by Mrs Elizabeth Smithers who also owned the forge a short distance away in the same row of houses. The shop window is remembered for all the copper kettles which seem to have been a speciality and this business, including the forge, was run by her three sons. The gate opened into a passage which led to a collection of small houses backing on to the George Yard. Today, the shop is the premises of Mrs Margaret Bird, Secretarial Services.

Ashdown Bros in 1930, showing E.J. Ashdown outside his shop in New Romney High Street. This was a general ironmongers and sports outfitters and, in earlier times, saddle and harness manufacturers, with all accessories for the horse, as well as portmanteaus and every travelling requisite. The Ashdown family have traded in New Romney since 1770.

Burton's butcher's shop in 1910, with George Burton standing in his doorway in New Street, Lydd. He was a high class butcher, slaughtering on the premises, as was the custom. His son Edgar carried on the business until the Second World War, when Cliff Cole moved into the shop from one in Church Street. It is still a good butcher's today, run by the Quinney family.

The prize steer, *c.* 1912. This Sussex bullock had been bought from Ashford Market to be slaughtered at the rear of Frank Hughes' butcher's shop in Lydd High Street. Mr Hughes is shown posing with his steer outside the shop. The premises next door are The Beehive Inn, notorious in its day, especially when bare-knuckle prize fighting was popular.

Clark Stores, New Romney, seen here *c.* 1912, stood at the junction of High Street and Church Approach. Jesse Hobbs, the manager, is shown on the left. Clark was a family grocer and provision merchant, draper, hatter and outfitter. It also dealt in china, glass, boots and shoes, millinery and dressmaking. This business was sold to Henry Headley, grocer of Ashford, during the First World War and closed in 1980.

Central Café, Dymchurch. This was the largest and best equipped restaurant on Romney Marsh, with the capacity for six hundred diners. At the time this photograph was taken in about 1930 hot and cold luncheons could be bought for 1s 6d and special teas for one shilling. Board residence (bungalow accommodation) was two guineas a week. The owners were Apps Ltd from Ashford. The three waitresses shown are Kath Harding, Ivy Pope and Ivy Butler.

The post office, Ivychurch, *c.* 1908. Situated just outside the village, the post office was also a small general store and provided daily deliveries by horse and cart to all areas. The shop at that time belonged to Mr Ormond who, by the sign on the wall, sold Blue Cross Teas. In fact you could purchase most requirements of the day. Later the shop was bought by W.K. King who made several structural alterations to the building. The shop closed some years ago and is now a private home called Kent House.

The staff of New Romney post office get together for a group photograph in 1935, the postmen very smart in their uniforms. The ladies, looking demure in ordinary dress, ran the clerical side of the post office. The postmen from left to right are: Eddie Ralph, Cliff Waller, Teddy Castle, Don Ashdown, Percy Kennett (postmaster), Archie Boulden and Arthur Ashdown. The ladies from left to right are: Miss Ellis, Mrs Kennett and Miss Hayward.

Central Stores, Newchurch, pictured here in about 1925, was not very far from the Black Bull public house and is now known as Newchurch House Restaurant. Like most of the village stores it incorporated the post office. The trade signs show the variety of goods from Robinson's Starch to five signs of Empire Nut Brown tobacco, presumably a popular choice. The window displays bottles of various drinks, suggesting that this was also an off-licence. Mr Haynes was a familiar sight in his little Fordson Eight delivering around the district.

'The Oldest Shop', c. 1915. R. Hope's in the High Street, Dymchurch, now called 'Beat's', in 1967 claimed to be the oldest shop trading in Dymchurch, selling novelties, confectionery, ices, coffee and tea. The signs in our picture are advertising Finn's Lydd Aerated Waters, and Colebrook's Aerated Waters. A selection of postcards is on display while in the window are jars of sweets and sherbet.

Stapley's Stores, *c.* 1910. This is the house and shop that appeared in earlier photographs of Brookland High Street as being in the middle of the road. It was a busy grocery and draper's shop owned at this time by C. Clayton, who is shown in the doorway. The delivery horse and cart went to all the outlying farms and hamlets leaving the weekly order and taking that for the following week. The house and shop were demolished in the late fifties or early sixties.

The delivery of goods, part of the service given by all traders, was vital if you lived on the coast or 'out in the grounds'. The large house is The Grange at Lydd, looking very much the same today. The horse and cart belong to A. White, Grocer and Draper, the boy with his trade bike is from Mr Goble's Bakery, while the handcart is being pushed by the postman delivering the parcel post.

A line of shops at Littlestone in 1928. The first shop is C.A. Wiles & Co., Land and Estate Agent, who is shown in an early directory as a furniture dealer. Littlestone Tea Rooms, run by Miss Elizabeth Pierce, catered for visitors to the sands a little further down the road – could the occupants of the car be taking refreshments or are they planning to buy from Mr Wiles?

Grocer and coalmerchant, Brenzett, c. 1910. The family of J. Haisell, his wife seated, his six children and two young ladies as shop assistants, pose for a photograph in George Street, now part of the A259 to Ashford. This business served Brenzett, Snargate and Snave. The shop was owned later by Arthur Reeves and finally closed in the early 1960s.

The Military

Because of its Cinque Ports status and its strategic position close to the coast of France, Romney Marsh has a long association with the armed forces, including its own former Cinque Ports Volunteers which in time became the East Kent Volunteers. Records show that in 1592 both Lydd and New Romney had trained bands, and in 1730 there was big funeral turn-out on the death of James Pelham, 'Captain of ye Militia of Lydd', while in 1794 the New Romney Fencible Cavalry had a notable resident, Cholmeley Dering, as its commander.

Not until 1874, however, did the Regular Army set up home in the area with the establishment of a permanent camp at Lydd, which in the years since has brought a welcome measure of cash and jobs and training visits by a succession of regiments. Relations between the Army and the local population have always been excellent and continue so to this day.

Along at West Hythe, on the site of the infamous Brockman's Barn, where fierce battles took place between smugglers and revenue officers in 1745, there stands the solid-looking Grand Redoubt, still much in use by the Army.

The East Anglians coming down Station Road, Lydd, in 1910, having arrived by train. The horses pulling a general service wagon are leading the column.

The Horse Lines at Lydd in 1910. In the summer months up to two thousand horses could be found in the Horse Lines by the canvas bell tents and the Army huts known as 'Tin Town'. The tall building on the right is the camp water tower, and Lydd and its church can be seen in the background.

The Gun Park of the Siege Artillery in Lydd Camp, *c.* 1910. The men in their overalls are cleaning and maintaining the guns and carriages.

Returning to Lydd Camp, *c.* 1910. These Royal Artillery Territorials are returning to the camp after gun drill on the West Rype. There were four horses and four men to each gun team.

Gun practice on the Lydd Ranges, *c.* 1906. The Royal Garrison Artillery are shown firing 4.7 in. guns out to sea. The men and ammunition would have been carried into position on the general service wagon seen beside each gun.

A military balloon observes the effects of shell fire, c. 1906. The Royal Artillery used balloons and kites on the practice range at Lydd, where it was quite usual to see these large objects with a man suspended in a basket underneath. The captive balloons, as they were called, were normally used for observation purposes unless winds were too strong, when kites had to be brought into action. The balloon was filled with hydrogen and ascended to about 500 ft.

Three men in a kite, c. 1906. When strong winds were blowing the kites came into use for observation purposes. These were mounted on wagons drawn by horses, with drums carrying the wire and means for control of winding in or out. Small lifting kites were sent up first, then the man-lifting kite with a basket and the observing officer in it with his instruments to observe the line of fire. Apart from a certain amount of swaying action, I am told the experience of observing from the kite was not unpleasant unless the cable snapped, as it did on one occasion. Fortunately nobody was seriously injured. Some of the finest aerial photographs of this area were taken by the enterprising Mr Shaw from a kite. This photograph is, of course, posed by other ranks, the actual work always being done by a single officer.

A detachment of the 107 Company, Royal Garrison Artillery, in 1908, with a 9.45 in. howitzer at Lydd Camp. These howitzers were made by the Skoda works of Czechoslovakia, and were originally purchased by the Army for use in the South African War, if necessary, against Pretoria. Some of the buildings of the permanent camp are shown in the background.

Observation of fire from the ground in 1913. The men seen here are having training in the use of instruments from a general service wagon, or a raised platform on the ranges for observing the firepower.

Civic Parade in 1909 outside the Guild Hall, Lydd. The Garrison Artillery line up after a church parade. Other regiments are seen coming out of the church to line up and march back to camp, a usual occurrence on a Sunday morning.

Marching across the West Rype in 1908. The troops normally used this route because the entrance to the camp was about 500 yards nearer the Dengemarsh Road than is the present camp entrance. In the background are the thatched cottage of Barton Gower the wheelwright, York House and Holmstone Terrace.

L Company, The 1st Volunteer Battalion, East Kent Regiment (The Buffs). This photograph was taken in 1895 in the garden of Elm Grove, Lydd, the home of the brewer Edwin Finn. It shows a fine body of men and it is a great pity that through time their names have been forgotten. However, we do know that the Commanding Officer was Major Harold Finn, and the instructor was Sergeant Adley.

No. 1 Battery, Dungeness, *c.* 1910. This had been built some time in the nineteenth century, replacing a previous fort on the site which had been used as a defence during the French and Napoleonic wars. The armament was four 24 lb cannon, later modified to take four 68 lb guns. In 1794 Captain Samuel Finn of Westbroke, of the Lydd Volunteers, was appointed barrack master. The battery was last used by the military in the Second World War and was also a storage area for PLUTO. (Pipe Line Under The Ocean was a submarine fuel pipeline that carried petrol under the Channel to the Allied forces in Normandy following D-Day in 1944.) Apart from a gun emplacement the battery was demolished by Kent County Council because they considered it an eyesore.

Romney Marsh Territorials, a detachment of the Cinque Ports Fortress Company, *c*. 1936. Recruitment was mainly local, and HQ was at St Mary's Bay. As war looked imminent, the defence of our coasts was paramount and the detachment became 468 Searchlight Company, Royal Engineers. Those pictured are, left to right, back row: D. Hall, J. Oiller, B. Browning, J. Rhodes, E. Burgess; middle row: C. Cheeseman Jnr, W. Longhurst, G. Paine, A. Flisher, E. Buckman, G. Broad; front row: C. Cheeseman Snr, E. Rigden, S. Taylor, W. Willicott, T. Burdett, S. Hall, P. Campbell.

First World War fort in 1920. This stood on the point at Dungeness, approximately where the new lighthouse stands. It was heavily armed and in the Second World War was part of the coastal defences under General Pile who paid it visits with Winston Churchill and General Smuts. The fort was demolished in the late 1950s.

The Grand Redoubt, West Hythe in 1912, viewed from Dymchurch. This circular fort, built at the beginning of the nineteenth century, stands on a man-made mound surrounded by a moat and has a commanding view of the Channel and any enemy approaching it. The site was previously that of the infamous Brockman's Barn, a smugglers' store and meeting place.

The Army Cadet Force in 1912. This Company is from Plaistow, near Haslemere in Surrey, having their photograph taken after giving a display to parents and local dignitaries in the Redoubt, Hythe. The chaplain and the instructors are in the centre, with the cadets in formation on the entrance stairs. Cadets trained and enjoyed themselves for two weeks and then would be replaced by another similar company from elsewhere in the south of England.

Plaistow Cadets at church service in 1912. Sunday parade was a regular feature at Hythe Redoubt, the portable altar and organ being kept there permanently. The casement quarters in their brick arches, with door and sash windows, each had a fireplace with chimney opening on to the moat. The Grand Redoubt today is still in the safe hands of the Ministry of Defence, which has a number of buildings of great historical value in its care.

Royal Flying Corps

An airfield was established at Lydd in 1913 and another at Jesson (now St Mary's Bay) in 1917. At Jesson the administrative buildings and living quarters were on the Romney side of Jesson Lane and the 75-acre airfield on the Dymchurch side. It was the base for No. 3 School of Aerial Gunnery, working and training with the Army at Shorncliffe and Lydd. Then, in 1919, the school moved to Manston and Jesson was used for emergency landing only, finally closing just before the outbreak of the Second World War.

Lydd, which closed with the signing of the Armistice in 1918 and reverted to farmland, provided a base at various times to Nos 3, 5, 6 and 112 Squadrons. Among the few flying accidents reported were a crash at Seabrook, a forced landing at Westbroke and a deliberate 'pancake' at Dungeness, all without casualties. But on 28 November 1917 Lieutenants Miller and Farrier were killed when their plane crashed and caught fire on the site of what is now the new Lydd cemetery.

The quarters of the Royal Flying Corps and the Balloon School, Dering Farm, Lydd, in 1913. The present track to Dering Farm runs between the first and second lines of huts shown. The gates to the Glebe can be seen at the entrance from Dennes Lane (top left) and the Lodge House (top right), with the YMCA canteen on the roadside.

Advanced Balloon School, Lydd, in 1915. This training unit was part of the RFC at Dering Farm. Although they were issued with thirty-nine balloons, only five could be used at any one time to train the observers and the winch and filling crews. An observer was taught to assess the enemy's fire and report its position to the guns. Suspended 800 ft in the air, he was an obvious target; nevertheless only one gun was allocated in defence, and in a dire emergency each observer had a parachute! The photograph shows a Drachen balloon ascending at Dering Farm.

Aircrew of the RFC, Lydd, in 1914. At this time the RFC was made up of both Army and Navy and included the women's services. Although they all had the same uniform they were allowed to use the badge of their own original regiment. One daily duty, whatever the weather, was to climb Lydd Church tower and measure the wind speed.

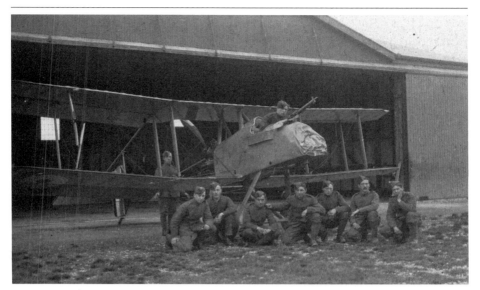

An early warplane at Lydd, *c.* 1916. Opinions have differed as to which type of aircraft this is, but·it is possibly a Vickers FB5 Gunbus. It was a pusher-type aircraft, with the engine at the rear. We do know, however, that it has been in some sort of accident, hence the crumpled nacelle and the broken strut. The armament is a Lewis gun.

A Horace Farman at Lydd Aerodrome, *c.* 1914. This was a French-designed pusher aircraft by Henri and Maurice Farman and had all the characteristics of their earlier types; it was chiefly used for reconnaissance work. As with all pushers, the observer sat in the front cockpit and the pilot behind; note the machine gun in the front cockpit. The rings in the ground are for anchoring the aircraft in strong winds.

An RE8 at Lydd, *c.* 1917. The aircraft was affectionately termed the 'Harry Tate' in rhyming slang, after the music-hall comedian of that name. The camera shown is the F1 made by Williamson and used in the Middle East in 1916. It was the first aerial reconnaissance camera to use film that was fully automatic, the slipstream from the aircraft providing the power to advance the film inside the camera. The RE8 was used in 1917–18 for reconnaissance and artillery spotting.

A group of BE2Cs of No. 3 Squadron RFC at Lydd in 1915. The first aeroplane is an earlier production BE2C with a Renault engine and a skid-type undercarriage. The other three are the Standard engine of 90 hp. These four aircraft flew from Jesson aerodrome to monitor the gunnery experiments at Hythe and Shorncliffe, as well as from Lydd for gunnery trials. The cost of a BE2C in the First World War was just under £2,000.

A naval airship over Lydd, *c*. 1916. This type of craft was used mainly for convoy escort work and submarine spotting. In the Services they acquired the name of 'Blimp', for airships came in two types: 'A' rigid, and 'B' limp. The gondola is a disused aeroplane fuselage.

Who'd be in his shoes! The young airman at Dering Farm, Lydd, is holding two Hale bombs as used by the RFC around 1915. On the left is a 20 lb Hale HE, the one on the right a 16 lb version. These bombs were hand released from the aircraft, being made live by the airflow acting upon rotating vanes. These vanes in turn unscrewed a safety screw from the detonator internal housing which was held back from a needle striker solely by the conical spring. On impact with a target, inertia forced the detonator capsule on to its striker, causing the bomb to explode.

Mr A. Ogilvie with his aeroplane at Camber in 1910. Ogilvie built his own aircraft in a large building in the sand dunes at Camber, having had a 15-inch gauge railway track laid to assist the plane on to the sands from which he took off. He took part in several air races, a popular sport at that time.

A Wight Seaplane at Rye Harbour in 1914. This unusual seaplane, built by John Samuel White & company of East Cowes, Isle of Wight, was powered by a 200 hp Salmson water-cooled Pusher engine. Eleven of these planes were eventually made, ten going to the Admiralty, while one was supplied to Germany. They were not very successful because they could not be relied on to take off from a choppy sea. Three of these seaplanes were based at Dover, including this one, No. 894. It ran into trouble and put down in the Rother and was towed to the slipway for repairs. The boy with the bicycle is Ernest Rook.

SECTION FOURTEEN
Dungeness Lighthouses

Dungeness, headland to the Romney Marshes, nourished by the ceaseless drift of shingle from the west, has ever been a danger point for Channel shipping. As long ago as 20 August 1615, after much agitation by mariners, a coal-fired beacon was installed and a toll of one penny per ton levied on all ships passing it. On 9 October 1635 this was replaced by a 110-ft tower much nearer the sea, but again with simply a fire on the top.

Then, in 1776, Thomas Coke – Coke of Norfolk – was given permission to build an Eddystone-type lighthouse, 116 ft high which, when completed in 1792 at a cost of £3,159 0s 4d, was lit first by sperm-oil lamps, next by electricity, and finally by paraffin. One hundred years later the sea had receded so much that the tower was 500 yd from the coastline and on 31 March 1904 a new lighthouse 136 ft high took its place, with a pressurized paraffin lamp of 164,000 candlepower which could be seen for 17 miles.

A picture taken in 1890 of Dungeness lighthouse.

Completion of the 1904 lighthouse at Dungeness. Over the years the sea had receded and therefore it was deemed necessary to replace the 1792 lighthouse which by then stood 500 yd from the sea. This new light was built for Trinity House by Pattrick & Co. of London, using a lot of local labour. The positioning of the present nuclear power stations impeded this light and consequently a new design lighthouse was built and began its noble work on 20 November 1961.

SECTION FIFTEEN

Wrecks and Rescues

Over the past two hundred years, hundreds of vessels have been wrecked along the Romney Marsh coast and hundreds of lives lost or put in peril. That the human toll has not been even higher is due to the fact that the men of the coast have ever been prepared not only to risk, but also to give, their own lives to save others. And still today the lifeboats of Dungeness and Littlestone are kept busy, though mainly because of the increase in leisure water sports.

Some lifeboat history has been lost in the passage of time and some has become confused, but memorial windows in churches and graves in churchyards bear witness to many of the earlier sea tragedies. At Littlestone the coastguard watchhouse, with its boathouse beneath, reminds one of the part the coastguard once played in manning the lifeboats.

The coastguards of Dengemarsh station are here photographed in 1895 with John Russell, on the left of his daughter, outside The Hope & Anchor inn, Dengemarsh. Mr Russell was the Commissioners' Overseer for the Denge Marsh Level. The coastguard at this time were part of the Royal Navy and during August naval training took place, the men here having just returned from Chatham.

Master Spry and friend, *c.* 1912. Young Spry was the son of the Chief Boatman-in-Charge at No. 3 Coastguard Station, Dengemarsh, and is here seen with the coastguard donkey, as issued to all remote stations which used such animals to draw the cart for obtaining provisions and fuel from the nearest village. The boy is seen here wearing 'backstays', wooden boards cut to the length of the shoe and about 6 inches wide with a leather strap which slips over the shoe. These were used for negotiating the shingle, and still are by some locals.

The Littlestone coastguard watch house, *c.* 1870. This picture was taken before all the holiday resort development began around 1885, when the watch house, the lifeboat station and the low tarred cottages of the coastguard were the only buildings. The watchroom gave a good view of the Channel, from Folkestone to Dungeness, and below was the boathouse where the galley was kept ready for any problems at sea such as checking boats for security reasons or smuggling. This galley was also used for rescues at sea should the lifeboat already be out, or should sea conditions favour a smaller boat. The watch house today is now a private house and has remained structurally unaltered since this photograph was taken.

The members of the Rocket Apparatus Company, Lade, in 1893. There were several companies placed at strategic positions on the Marsh coast. Often the only hope of rescue for crews from wrecked vessels was by breeches buoy, needing skill to fire a line aboard to bring men safely to shore. From left to right, back row: John Oiller, ? Foster, Robin Tart, Jim Roper, -?-; middle row: Toby Oiller, Harry Reeves, Jim Oiller, John Ramsen Coastguard-in-Charge, Harry Young, George Reeves, Herbert Oiller; front row: Joe Oiller, Steven Foster, Harry Wood-Brignall, ? Richardson, -?-.

New Romney/Littlestone lifeboat, *The Sandal Magna*, *c.* 1898, on its carriage drawn by Carey's horses going to New Romney for Lifeboat Day. The lifeboat would be paraded round the streets with the crew and helpers collecting money. The crew are wearing the then new kapok life jacket which had replaced the cork jacket.

A gallant rescue crew, pictured in 1891. On 11 November 1891 a severe storm lashed the coast of Britain with hurricane force winds, and many vessels were wrecked. At first light coastguards and local fishermen were summoned from their beds to man the rocket lifesaving apparatus to aid the *Marguerite Marie*, in trouble near Littlestone. The crew were brought ashore safely. A second ship, *Domin of Arundel* was on her side and breaking up and, although the rocket crew rescued two men, all others were lost. Meanwhile a Swedish Brigantine *Aeolus* was on a sandbank off Littlestone with a crew of eight. The Dungeness Lifeboat, the RAOB, being the weather boat, was launched in appalling conditions and reached the stricken vessel but a tremendous sea caught her and she capsized with the loss of two lifeboatmen. A crew for the Littlestone boat could not be found, except for the coxswain and 2nd coxswain, but a fisherman from Dungeness, Isaac Tart, took the initiative to form a crew and they walked the mile along the beach to Littlestone. After many attempts they succeeded in launching and carried out a successful rescue, bringing the crew of eight safely to shore. The King of Sweden presented medals to the crew, as did Lloyds of London. Standing, left to right: 2nd Coxswain Cg (coastguard) Walker, Cg Goff, Fishermen Charles Oiller and Robin Tart, Lydd resident Alex Proctor, Coxswain Cg Clifton, Fisherman Isaac Tart and the Revd C.A.W. Robbins, Curate of Lydd. Seated: Cg Horton, Cg O'Leary, Dungeness man George Richardson, and Cg Cowell.

The crew and helpers at Littlestone in 1900, standing in front of their new lifeboat, *James Stevens No. 11*. This was a larger lifeboat than previously, so a new lifeboat house and carriage were supplied. During her service she carried out five recorded rescues, saving twenty-seven lives. It is interesting to note that in the photograph the crew are wearing a mixture of life-jackets, some kapok and others the old cork jackets. Many lifeboatmen were very reluctant to give up the cork jackets on which they had relied for so many years.

Launching of *The Harry Wright Russell*, *c.* 1925. The lifeboat here is being launched from a slipway rather than from a carriage. This new boat arrived at Littlestone on 12 August 1912 and the christening ceremony was performed on 1 October by the Revd H.G. South of New Romney. She was launched only on three services and moved to Hythe when Littlestone station was closed in 1928. In 1966 the RNLI opened Littlestone station again, with an inshore lifeboat.

The *Thomas Simcox*, the No. 2 lifeboat,
Dungeness, *c.* 1895. At the time this was the
largest lifeboat in service with the RNLI.
When she first arrived in 1892 it was decided
to keep her permanently afloat, but because
of the sea conditions on this part of the coast
it proved difficult for crews to board her. The
photograph shows her on the beach, waiting
for the call.

Experiments of launching from a railway track, Dungeness, *c.* 1895. It was hoped that
by using a carriage, designed to be used on a railway track, the lifeboat could be
launched from two positions on the beach, depending on wind direction and sea
conditions. The weight of the *Thomas Simcox*, however, and the number of men
required to manhandle it, made this experiment unsuccessful.

The launch of the *Thomas Simcox* from Dungeness in 1912. This launch provided an impressive sight as the lifeboat hit the water, having slid down the wooden, greased skids on the steep beach-bank. Her masts are raised ready for the sails as she enters the water, and she is also fitted with twelve double-banked oars should they be needed. The *Thomas Simcox* was launched on service twelve times and saved thirty-three lives.

The last of the pulling and sailing lifeboats, 1920. This was the *David Barclay of Tottenham*, which came on station in 1915. At this time, also, it was decided to close the No. 1 lifeboat station which left the larger *David Barclay* to become known as Dungeness lifeboat station.

The first motor lifeboat at Dungeness, *c.* 1933, was named the *Charles Cooper Henderson*. In the picture the lifeboat is preparing to come ashore after a practice launch, helped by the women launchers. Dungeness was the last station to carry on the tradition of women launchers. The ex-Coxswain John Pope is the signalman. Altogether the *Charles Cooper Henderson* was launched 171 times and saved sixty-three lives, a proud record.

The crew of the *Charles Cooper Henderson* in 1933. From left to right: Coxswain D. Oiller, 2nd Coxswain J. Oiller, R. Tollard, RNLI, P. Oiller, T.R. Tart Snr., G. Tart, J. Oiller, J. Brignall, W. Brignall, F. Oiller. In 1947 Coxswain Doug Oiller retired after thirty-one years as coxswain at Dungeness, his place being taken by George Tart who had joined the crew in 1924.

The wreck of the Norwegian barque *Jarlen of Mors* in 1891, which had been on passage between Pensacola and Rotterdam, carrying a cargo of pitch pine. A severe gale was blowing from the west and the *Jarlen* had run into a sandbank off Lade. The Littlestone lifeboat *Sandal Magna* was launched and by the skill of Coxswain Clifton succeeded in rescuing all on board including the captain's wife.

The steamship *Cragoswald* was driven ashore at Jury's Gap, *c.* 1904, after engine failure in a severe gale. Once the gale had abated the task of refloating the ship commenced, and a great deal of the cargo was unloaded and taken by horse and cart to Rye. Hundreds of empty barrels were buried under her hull and with this extra buoyancy and the aid of tugs she was refloated and towed into Rye Harbour.

The *Malpas Belle* refloated in 1909. It was on 8 January, just after midnight, that information was received that the master of the *Malpas Belle* required assistance. The Littlestone lifeboat *James Stevens No. 11* was launched and stood by. The *Malpas Belle* had been holed below the waterline on the starboard bow, her cargo of bags of cement was thrown overboard, and she was patched and refloated. These bags of cement can still be seen at Littlestone at very low water. This ill-fated vessel was destined to be sunk by a German U-boat in 1915.

Fire Brigades

Following a spate of fires in the town and surrounding district, and the nearest brigades being in Rye, Hythe and Ashford, Lydd decided in 1890 to have its own volunteer brigade, with a manually operated horse-drawn fire engine made by Merryweather & Sons of London, complete with 500 ft of hose.

In 1936 Camber formed its own brigade, purchasing an engine and building a station. Dymchurch also formed a brigade in 1935, buying a Leyland engine from the London Fire Brigade and appointing Sid Checksfield as captain.

The original crew of Lydd Volunteer Fire Brigade in 1890, outside their newly built fire station with their twenty-two man manual Merryweather fire engine. On the engine from left to right are: H. Maynard, Walter Haisell, Engineer G. Munds, Captain H. Finn, H.L. Cole and C. Cole; standing, left to right: W. Martin, 2nd Lieutenant G. Bishopp, F. Adams, 1st Lieutenant William Haisell.

Fighting a house fire in New Romney High Street in 1901. Mr George Allen's horses would have pulled the manual engine from Lydd post-haste. In the meanwhile a group of New Romney men attached to the Lydd Brigade, would hope to contain the fire until the arrival of the engine. Captain Harold Finn is directing operations while his four firemen fight the blaze.

The funeral of Fireman H. Allen, 1910. The cortège with the coffin, draped in the Union flag and carried on the fire engine, passes through Coronation Square, Lydd. It is led by Captain Harold Finn and followed by members of the Lydd Brigade, as well as colleagues from Rye, Hythe, Tenterden and Ashford.

The wedding of Percy King, fireman of Dymchurch, in 1936. The bridal party ride on the Leyland ex-London Fire Brigade engine. From left to right: Louis Henly, Percy Button, Jimmy Jones, ? Samson, Brian Francis (driver), Bride and Groom, Charlie Hoper and Chief Officer Sydney Checksfield.

The Silver Jubilee Procession in 1935. The Dennis fire engine of Lydd, driven by Percy Olver, leads the procession in celebration of King George V's Silver Jubilee. The engine always led processions so that, if necessary, they could answer emergency calls unimpeded.

Harry Smithers's farm fire in 1928. This was one of the biggest fires and is still remembered in Lydd today. Barns, buildings, straw and haystacks were destroyed by this devastating fire, although it had been attended by Lydd, Rye and Hythe Brigades assisted by the Army camp fire team. A strong wind from the west made it impossible to control matters satisfactorily.

A fire in the attic and roof of The Grand Hotel, Littlestone, c. 1936. This scene has been captured for us by a passing aeroplane. The fire was eventually brought under control, but a considerable amount of damage was caused. The large house on the left was the home of Sir Robert Perks of the South East & Chatham Railway. In the background are Charity Hall and the Roman Catholic Church.

SECTION SEVENTEEN
Listening Posts

Listening posts were known locally on the Romney Marsh as the 'Listening Walls'. These large concrete structures, standing on the beach at Greatstone were built and used over a period between 1922 and 1935. The idea behind the experiments was to be able to detect, by sound, aircraft approaching the English coast from Europe. They were to have been an early warning system to be used in case of war. Each one had a small control room with various microphones and instruments to detect sound. The cost outweighed their limited success and the project was abandoned. Locals in the area remember that when the Service chiefs came to see a demonstration it had been arranged for a plane to fly towards the listening post to test its efficiency. As they all gathered round, a buzz, then a drone and a rattling sound was heard, increasing in volume. Puzzlement was on all faces, until they looked up and saw the local milkman with rattling churns making his way along the track.

The largest Listening Post is almost 200 ft in length, with a row of microphones on the plinth. This sound wall was constructed using tons of concrete and the small track railway ran from the road to the quarters and stores.

The largest of the Bowl Reflectors. This edifice measuring 30 ft across stands on the beach near the other posts, but looks more like something from a science fiction film. As the shingle was constantly moving, repairs were repeatedly having to be carried out, usually by Bates of Lydd, later by Ellis Bros of New Romney.

The smallest of the Echo Mirrors. This had a large microphone capable of picking up sound from many miles away, but of course background noises intervened. These concrete reflectors can still be observed at Greatstone, but aggregates extraction close by has almost toppled one over. Nevertheless they are worth preserving as part of our history, even if they did not fulfil expectations.

SECTION EIGHTEEN
Sporting Activities

Marshmen, like their sheep, had to be pretty tough, and they worked hard and played hard – never more so than in the almost forgotten sport of goalrunning. This certainly dates beyond living memory and there are many myths as to its origin. For this pastime which was similar to cross-tag – and calling for fast runners, skill and cunning – most villages fielded a team and it seemed that many had their own set of rules, so games were lively, to say the least.

Football, cricket and tennis tournaments were held; so too were sports days, catering for all ages and sexes and there were cups and prizes to be won. The big event at Lydd was the mile race round the Rype, with notable local winners such as the 'Trotty' Holdstock family and Harry Allen, and always a strong challenge each year from the Army.

A fine body of men. Members of the Lydd Goal-Running Team, the winners in 1909 of the Tenterden Cup and the even more prized New Romney Cup. It is known that great rivalry still exists between New Romney and Lydd, this stemming mainly from the ancient sport of goalrunning. It is not possible to name the individual players, but the families of Baker, Finn, Marshall, Pope, Mackett, Holdstock and Wood are represented. The photograph was taken outside Finn's Brewery at Lydd.

Goalrunning Team, Dymchurch, in 1915. Back row, left to right: Mr Piddock, Fred Kemp, Harry Waddell, Ted Piper, Albert Woodland, Dick Trice, Arch Wraight, Ted Woodland, Percy Wood, Charlie Hoper, Bunky Simpson; middle row: Bill Piper, Jack Harris, Jim (Peggy) Flisher, Reg Wraight, George Ralph, Bill (Wackett) Rogers; front row: Horace (Punch) Piddock, Nobby Gates, Jumbo Coombs, Fred Austen, Fred Harris, Fred Waddell.

East Guldeford football team, in 1925. The hamlet of East Guldeford formed a team and played in the Rye and District League. Back row, left to right: -?-, Harry Neves, Bert Shepherd, Basil Baker, Bill Tolhurst, Ken Hickman; front row: Freddie Tolhurst, -?-, Bob Anderson, -?-, Reg Fairall.

Lydd Football Club, 1922–3 season. Back row left to right: Norman Balcomb, George Newton, Beckly Smith, Cecil Blacklocks, Tim Paine, Bill Marchant; middle row: Charlie Sisley, Bert Paine, Claude Paine (captain), C. Gurr, Harold Batchelor; front row: Bill Balchin and Tom Prebble.

'The Snowflakes', c. 1915. Perhaps the most unlikely place to form a football team would be Dungeness, all beach and no grass, but through the years, with the support of the coastguard, they have fielded a team widely known as 'The Snowflakes'. Back row, left to right: A. Freathy, Beefer Thomas, three coastguards, Frank Oiller, Raymond Oiller; middle row: Brignell, a coastguard, Doug Oiller; front row: John Oiller, Fred Tart and Joe Oiller.

The Mile Race, Lydd Sports Day, 1920. This event, which drew large crowds, was the main attraction at Lydd Sports Day. Competitors came from local towns and villages, from the Army camp and the coastguard. Lydd had some strong contenders, the family of Holdstock being nicknamed 'Trotties' for good reason. Harry Allen was also several times a winner early in the twentieth century.

Lydd Sports Day, 1920. This was also a children's day when races were organized with prizes for the winners. In the photograph the 100 yd final is taking place watched by the coastguard, the starter and, of course, the cheering crowd.

Brenzett Ladies' Cricket Team, *c.* 1935. The ladies of Brenzett are said to have not only had a very good team, but also to have taken the game very seriously. Back row left to right: -?-, Margaret Thompson, -?-, -?-, Daphne Unstead; middle row: Barb West, Kath Dines, Lil Hurst, Winnie Unstead; front row: Mrs Gosbee, Mrs Rummery and Kath Hovenden.

The Club House of Greatstone Golf Club, 1930. At this time the Club House stood in Station Road, New Romney, on the left-hand side going towards Littlestone. The eighteen-hole course was owned by Mr H.T. Tubbs. While the professional was repairing some clubs he was called away and left his glue pot on the fire. This boiled over and the Club House went up in flames.

The Littlestone Golf Course, *c.* 1900. After gathering a committee together in 1888, Henry Tubbs laid out at his own expense an eighteen-hole course on the land known as The Warren. In the picture the low tarred houses of the coastguard can be seen while to the left are Sandcroft and Sealands.

Littlestone Golf House, 1928. The Golf Club attracted many wealthy people to Littlestone and developers built large houses to encourage members to buy second homes in the area. The Tudor-style house on the right is nearing completion. The Golf House was built by Ellis Bros of New Romney and completed in 1901. A grand building, it has altered very little to this day.

SECTION NINETEEN
Field Sports

Today some field sports are the centre of controversy, but years ago they were widely accepted as part and parcel of the countryside. The John Jones Coursing Club, started in the second half of the nineteenth century by Farmer Jones, had permission it is said to ride and hunt over 15,000 acres of marshland, with greyhounds being matched in speed and endurance against hares.

In 1884 Albert Cock of Appledore, with Thomas Finn of Westbroke, Lydd, established a pack of hounds, the Romney Marsh Harriers, to hunt hares (foxes were rare on Romney Marsh until the Second World War). The hare was also the quarry for the Marsh Beagles, a New Romney pack, who followed on foot.

The 3rd Battalion, Royal Tank Corps, kept a pack – seven and a half couples of Basset Hounds – at Lydd in 1926, hunting hares on Tuesdays and Fridays with, as Master, Lieutenant-Colonel Frederick Pile, later to become General Sir Frederick Pile, GCB, DSO, MC, General Officer Commanding Anti-Aircraft Command in the Second World War.

A meeting of the John Jones Coursing Club, *c.* 1915. The owners or handlers are holding their couples in pairs, preparatory to being conveyed by a closed cart to chosen fields, perhaps Dengemarsh, to pit the speed and wits of the hounds against the hares.

The Romney Marsh Harriers in 1920, meeting at the Old Red Lion in The Street at Appledore. The joint masters with the hounds are Mr R.W. Stent and Lieutenant-Colonel G.W. Liddell. At the time of the photograph the hunt consisted of seventeen couples made up of dwarf foxhound and harrier bitches.

The Romney Beagles, *c.* 1910. This pack is seen outside High House, High Street, New Romney, the home of the Revd Hugh South (in the doorway) who was a keen field sportsman and patron of the beagle pack. The pack was taken to quarter most parts of the Marsh for hares.

Festivities and Entertainments

During the year every centre of population on Romney Marsh would hold some sort of jollification – perhaps a village or church fête, or something larger like Club Days, which took place at Brenzett and Lydd. Coronations and other royal occasions also made days to remember.

A more formal event was Hospital Sunday, when a church service would be followed by a procession round the town by all the clubs and organizations, making house-to-house collections for the local hospitals. Summer Sundays in Lydd were lent colour by the Army. Territorials in camp, and the resident garrison, would march to church headed by their bands, and would return to camp escorted by local residents all in their Sunday best, scurrying ahead or following behind. Sometimes the day was rounded off by a band concert in Coronation Square in the evening.

Although all town and village festivities were lubricated by glasses of Finn's Lydd Ales, little trouble or hooliganism resulted.

New Romney Town Band, *c.* 1915. This was the well-known and popular band which played at most local events. They were also called upon for ceremonial occasions such as church parades and Hospital Sunday. The nearest band to Romney Marsh today is at Hythe.

The proclamation of King George V at Lydd, in 1910. From left to right: Mr W. Hook, Captain of the Fire Brigade Harold Finn, John Lever, Joe Goble, W. Green, George Bishop, Mayor Edwin Finn, William Blacklocks, Arthur Finn, Fireman H.L. Cole, the Town Sergeant Barr Flisher, with Army in attendance.

East Guldeford celebrates the Coronation of King George V, in 1911. For this fête and fun day everybody in the hamlet would help to make it a day to remember, and the photograph indicates the tremendous effort put in to guarantee success. We see winners in the decorated pram competition, from left to right: Mrs W. Webb second prize, Mrs J. Hickman first prize, and Mrs H. Wilson extra prize.

Lydd's Jubilee celebrations in 1935. To help Lydd celebrate the Silver Jubilee of George V, a Jubilee Queen was to be elected and a line of hopeful young ladies are shown awaiting the judges' decision. Unfortunately Dorothy Lepper, who was elected, is not shown here, but we have, from left to right: Joan Smithers, Peggy Marshall, Kath Williams, Vera Marcrett, Betty Spanner, Dorothy Miller, Joyce Smith, and Sylvia Oliver.

The Duke of Kent's visit to New Romney in 1937. The duke is here seen talking to the Mayor, Major M. Teichman Derville, while left is the Mayor of Lydd, Mr G.T. Paine. Mace bearers in attendance are Mr Miller, right, and Mr Jocky Piper facing the camera. The lady taking the photographs is Councillor Mrs Terry.

The Duke of York visiting St Mary's Bay holiday camp in 1926. In the early 1920s the Duke of York started this summer camp to encourage boys from public schools and the inner cities to mix together and break down social barriers. He is here seen with the resident Camp Chief, Captain J.O. Paterson.

Boys enjoying their stay at camp, *c.* 1930. This was quite an adventure for many of the boys, possibly the first time many had visited the countryside. Games and events were well organized, and the sea was a great attraction.

St Mary's Bay holiday camp from the air. This was originally the Aerial School of Gunnery and the buildings used by the holiday camp were at one time accommodation for the airmen. The field on the top right of the picture was the aerodrome, while the house nestling in the trees was the home of Mopper Apps, the looker and shearer already featured in this book.

Hospital Sunday in New Romney, *c.* 1920. A procession of local council and dignitaries on their way to the service in St Nicholas Church, accompanied by many inhabitants dressed for the occasion. The banner is that of Victoria Hospital, Folkestone.

The Lydd Fire Brigade with its New Romney members, and the crew of the Littlestone lifeboat, *c.* 1920, take their part in the Hospital Day parade at New Romney.

Children of Dungeness attend a service at the Dungeness Mission Room, *c.* 1912. The Methodists held a well-attended service every Sunday morning in the old No. 1 Battery, the parson journeying from Lydd for this purpose. Tea and cakes were provided by the helpers and parents. The children very often then attended the Church of England Sunday School at the old school in the afternoon, and the church service in the evening.

The annual church fête in the grounds of Elm Grove, Lydd, *c.* 1912. The vicar, the Revd P.H. Collins, is here with his churchwardens and parishioners, possibly giving a blessing as all are looking solemn for what should be a festive occasion.

Band concert in Coronation Square, Lydd, *c.* 1912. After evensong on a summer evening whichever regiment was in residence at Lydd Camp would play for the entertainment of the locals. The Buffs are shown on this occasion.

The jazz band of the Garrison Artillery, 1919. A few locals are joining in the entertainment provided by this Army band which was often found playing outside the various public houses in Lydd. These are seen turning the corner by The Royal Oak, Lydd, captured by the camera of Mr A.E. Shaw.

A Dungeness picnic in 1906. The newly completed lighthouse can be seen in the background of this family group who would have travelled, possibly by rail, to enjoy the sea air. The fire is prepared for a cup of tea, with billy cans ready for suspending from the hook. These cans were the type normally used to carry water to bedrooms. From left to right: Sarah Body, Master Finn, Maggie Finn with baby, Dorothy Jane Body, Bertha Lansdell Body, and other members of the Finn family.

Brookland Chapel anniversary, 1905. One of the enjoyable events in the Methodist calendar was and still is the local chapel anniversary, with a special service to which other chapels are invited. Certainly, this picture shows a congregation very much dressed up for the occasion.

Lydd Club Day, 1907. The big social event at Lydd was the annual Club Day organized by the Friendly Clubs, the Enrolled, the Foresters and the Oddfellows. A dinner was held, also a concert where the general public could show off their talents. Meanwhile great fun would be had at the fair on the Rype. The photograph shows the steam switchback owned by Fred Macklin.

Brenzett Club Day, 1909. While obviously not as big an event as Lydd Club Day, this was another very important festive occasion, calling for new or at least best clothes, and treats were the order of the day. The central pole is attracting young men and youths to try their strength in an attempt to ring the bell and impress their contemporaries.

Church Parade, Lydd, 1911. After the Sunday morning church service, bands would accompany the troops on their return to camp, and the populace would enjoy the entertainment of accompanying the marching men, and demonstrating a feeling of rapport with the Army. During the summer months, with more than one regiment at Lydd, this became very much a special Sunday occasion with every man and boy in hat and tie, all ladies and girls in festive attire, the older children caring for their younger brothers and sisters. They may have been less well off in 1909, but there was no lack of pride then.

A dancing bear in New Romney High Street, 1913. I don't really think one could call this entertainment, but it was not uncommon at that date to find performing animals being exploited as money-making ventures. This particular bear was made to dance by being prodded with a stick, while a man played an accordion. A bear was kept at this period by the Canadian Army which had a camp on the right, just before you enter Lydd from New Romney, an area then known as The Canadian Gorse, now the site of a quarry.

Five local lads take part in a donkey race at Brenzett, *c.* 1909. This could have been a local Club Day or church fête as tents and stalls can be seen in the background. Two of the lads are wearing rosettes, previous winners, perhaps? From left to right: Jesse Fielder, Victor Beard, Frank Moore, Alf Williams and ? Upton.

The Old Police Station at Lydd, 1910. The small towns each had three policemen and most villages had one. In all the entertainments shown the police had very little trouble, even with thousands of troops who attended most of the activities in all the villages. Lydd police had two cells, but as far as we know these were not used until the Second World War when two German spies were held there for a short period.

Acknowledgements

I would like to express my gratitude to John Edwards for allowing me to select from his extensive collection of photographs. Also, I would especially like to thank Harry Cawkell and Hilda Evans who gave up their valuable time to read and correct the draft.

My thanks also to the following for information, advice, and their kind hospitality: Mr & Mrs M. Allen, Dick Body, Mr & Mrs G. Bone, Ernie Burgess, Mr & Mrs D. Cole, Dave Ford, Mr & Mrs S. Goodsell, John Henley, Mrs P. Kemp, Mr & Mrs J.D. Lowrie, Mr Dave Mattock, Mr & Mrs H. Pierce, Mr & Mrs Jim Pilcher, Mr & Mrs Joe Pilcher, Mr & Mrs H. Prebble, Mr & Mrs T. Standen, Bill Southerden, Mr & Mrs T.R. Tart, Mr D.B. Tubbs and Lt-Col Mike Umbers. My appreciation goes also to the photographers Peter Chillingworth and Brian Hebditch for their valuable work. Most importantly my thanks go to my wife Chris and my immediate family for all their encouragement and support.

In particular I must express my appreciation for the loan of photographs as follows (the numbers refer to pages, 'a' and 'b' to upper and lower respectively):

D. Arter, 136a; J. Ashdown, 98b; R. Body, 151b, 155a, and 74a; W. Burgess, 112; D. Cole, 86b; M. Cooper, 111a; P. Copson, 127a; G. Couchman, 83a; G. Durrant, 91b; J. Edwards, 6, 10a, 13b, 14a, 15a, 15b, 18, 19b, 20b, 21a, 21b, 22a, 22b, 23, 25a, 25b, 30a, 30b, 31a, 31b, 32b, 34a, 34b, 36a, 36b, 37b, 40a, 40b, 41b, 42a, 42b, 50a, 50b, 53b, 54b, 65b, 69b, 70b, 81a, 83b, 84a, 84b, 89a, 91a, 93b, 95b, 99a, 99b, 101a, 102a, 103b, 104a, 105b, 106a, 106b, 107a, 107b, 109b, 110a, 110b, 113b, 114a, 114b, 125b, 127b, 134b, 136b, 140a, 142a, 142b, 143b, 144a, 146a, 147b, 151a, 152a, 152b, 156b and 159b; J. Elgar-Whinney, 137a, 137b, 138a and 138b; G. Elvy, 64; D. Ford, 82a; E. Freathy, 48a, 71b, and 72b; Friends of Lydd, 72a, 116a, 117a, 117b, 118a, 118b, 119a and 119b. S. Goodsell, 135a; J. Henley, 70a, 102b and 151b; P. Hill, 150; F. Hobbs, 24a, 24b, 90a, 90b, 92b, 100a, 101b and 158; T. Keenan, 86a; J. Knight, 155b; D. & S. Mattock, 27b and 88b; A. Paine, 16b, 58a, 76a and 78a; J. Pilcher, 57b, 60a, 61b, 69a, 76b, 78b, 85a, 85b, 87b, 140b and 148b; E. Prebble, 48b, 56a and 73a; H. Prebble, 66a, 128a and 129a; M. Rook, 120b; M. Smith, 32a and 100b; the late W. Smith of Ashford, 45a, 104b, 143a, and 159a; T.R. Tart, 47b, 52a, 55, 56b, 74b, and 141b; P. Tidd, 63a. All the remaining photographs are from the author's own collection.